Cambridge Elements ≡

Elements in Philosophy of Mind
edited by
Keith Frankish
The University of Sheffield

NEUROLAW

Gregg D. Caruso
SUNY Corning

CAMBRIDGE
UNIVERSITY PRESS

Shaftesbury Road, Cambridge CB2 8EA, United Kingdom

One Liberty Plaza, 20th Floor, New York, NY 10006, USA

477 Williamstown Road, Port Melbourne, VIC 3207, Australia

314–321, 3rd Floor, Plot 3, Splendor Forum, Jasola District Centre,
New Delhi – 110025, India

103 Penang Road, #05–06/07, Visioncrest Commercial, Singapore 238467

Cambridge University Press is part of Cambridge University Press & Assessment,
a department of the University of Cambridge.

We share the University's mission to contribute to society through the pursuit of
education, learning and research at the highest international levels of excellence.

www.cambridge.org
Information on this title: www.cambridge.org/9781009500425

DOI: 10.1017/9781009271172

First published 2024

A catalogue record for this publication is available from the British Library.

ISBN 978-1-009-50042-5 Hardback
ISBN 978-1-009-27115-8 Paperback
ISSN 2633-9080 (online)
ISSN 2633-9072 (print)

Cambridge University Press & Assessment has no responsibility for the persistence
or accuracy of URLs for external or third-party internet websites referred to in this
publication and does not guarantee that any content on such websites is, or will
remain, accurate or appropriate.

Neurolaw

Elements in Philosophy of Mind

DOI: 10.1017/9781009271172
First published online: February 2024

Gregg D. Caruso
SUNY Corning

Author for correspondence: Gregg D. Caruso, gcaruso@corning-cc.edu

Abstract: Neurolaw is an area of interdisciplinary research on the meaning and implications of neuroscience for the law and legal practices. This Element addresses the potential contributions of neuroscience, and the brain sciences more generally, to criminal justice decision-making and policy. It distinguishes between three different areas and domains of investigation in neurolaw: assessment, intervention, and revision. The first concerns brain-based assessments, which may be used for predicting future violence, lie detection, judging legal insanity, and the like. The second concerns potential treatments and other interventions that aim at rehabilitating criminals and/or preventing crime before it occurs. The third investigates the ways that neuroscience may impact the law by changing or revising commonsense views about human nature and the causes of human action.

Keywords: neurolaw, neuroscience, law, criminal punishment, neurointerventions, responsibility, free will

ISBNs: 9781009500425 (HB), 9781009271158 (PB), 9781009271172 (OC)
ISSNs: 2633-9080 (online), 2633-9072 (print)

Contents

1 Neurolaw   1

2 Assessment   10

3 Intervention   33

4 Revision   47

   References   67

1 Neurolaw

Neurolaw is an area of interdisciplinary research on the meaning and implications of neuroscience for the law and legal practices. It encompasses not only the study of the neural workings of the human brain as they relate to issues of crime, guilt, and punishment, but also the emerging applications of imaging technologies within courtroom proceedings. As a field of study, neurolaw investigates the application of neuroscientific findings and techniques, along with their implications, in developing more accurate methods for lie detection and criminal behavior prediction, developing more effective means of criminal rehabilitation, and improving sentencing procedures. A core aim of neurolaw is to provide a scientific foundation for understanding human behavior, leading to more informed and fair legal practices and policies.

This Element addresses the potential contributions of neuroscience and the brain sciences, more generally, to criminal justice decision-making and policy. It begins by distinguishing between three different areas and domains of investigation in neurolaw: assessment, intervention, and revision (Morse and Roskies 2013; Meynen 2014).[1] The first concerns brain-based *assessments*, which may be used for predicting future violence, lie detection, judging legal insanity, and the like. The second concerns potential treatments and other *interventions* that aim at rehabilitating criminals and/or preventing crime before it occurs. The third investigates the ways that neuroscience may impact the law by changing or *revising* "commonsense views about human nature and the causes of human action" (Morse and Roskies 2013: 241).

While it's impossible to cover everything in a short survey like this, the goal of this Element is to provide readers with an opinionated introduction to the main issues and debates within neurolaw. This section provides a brief overview of the three domains just mentioned, with the aim of explaining why and in what ways neuroscience may be relevant to the law and legal practice. Subsequent sections then examine the ethical and legal issues associated with each domain in more detail.

1.1 Neurolaw: A Brief Introduction

The 1990s were designated the "decade of the brain" by President George H.W. Bush and the US Congress. This period was marked by an extraordinary increase in the visibility of neuroscience and a renewed interest in the localization of neural phenomena to distinct anatomical regions of the brain. The rapid

---

[1] This tripart classification was first proposed by Morse and Roskies (2013) and subsequently adopted by Meynen (2014). I adopt it here since it provides a clear and natural way to classify the different domains of neurolaw.

growth of functional magnetic resonance imaging (fMRI) research, for instance, led to new insights into neuroanatomical structure and function, which, in turn, led to a greater understanding of human behavior and cognition. In response to these developments, questions emerged regarding how these findings can be applied to criminology and legal processes. As Martin Roth describes, "The last two decades have seen an explosion of interest in what impact, if any, our growing knowledge of the brain will or should have for legal theory and practice" (2018: 1). The field of study that has developed around this interest is now commonly referred to as "neurolaw."

Neurolaw is an interdisciplinary field that involves collaboration between neuroscientists, legal scholars, psychologists, and ethicists. Its goal is to bridge the gap between neuroscience and the law, providing a scientific foundation for informed legal decision-making. By "neuroscience," I include not only those areas of research that study the brain directly (its structures, functions, developments, and abnormalities), but also those that study behavioral genetics and cognition more generally. I, therefore, interpret the "neuro" part of *neurolaw* rather broadly.

The term "neurolaw" was first coined by Taylor, Harp, and Elliot (1991) in a *Neuropsychology* journal article analyzing the role of psychologists and lawyers in the criminal justice system. After its publication, scholars began networking, organizing conferences, and publishing books and articles about the intersection of neuroscience and law. The developing field of neurolaw was then given a boost by the initiation of the Law and Neuroscience Project by The MacArthur Foundation. Phase 1 of this project was launched in 2007 with a $10 million grant. The initiative sustained forty projects addressing a multitude of issues, including experimental and theoretical data that explored how neuroscience may eventually shape the law. Since then, a number of universities have developed neurolaw centers dedicated to exploring the social, legal, and ethical implications of neuroscience.

Neurolaw is closely aligned with, and developed in parallel with, *neuroethics* (see Roskies 2002, 2021; Levy 2007, 2012). Neuroethics is a sub-discipline of philosophy with two broad focuses. The first, which has come to be called the *ethics of neuroscience*, concerns the assessment of ethical issues arising from neuroscience, its practice, and its applications; the second, which has come to be called the *neuroscience of ethics*, concerns the ways in which the sciences of the mind can illuminate longstanding issues within philosophy (Levy 2012: 143). The ethics of neuroscience deals, for instance, with concerns about the application of fMRI-based lie detection systems in forensic settings and ethical considerations raised in the course of designing and executing neuroscientific studies. The neuroscience of ethics, on the other hand, deals with the degree to which we might be required to revise folk or philosophical conceptions of the self in the light of work in cognitive neuroscience. As Adina Roskies explains, "Traditional ethical theory has centered on philosophical notions such as free will, self-control, personal identity, and intention. These notions [however] can [now] be investigated from the perspective of brain function" (2002: 22). This, Roskies predicts, will have "profound implications for the way ethics, writ large, is approached in the 21st century" (2002: 22).

While there is some controversy over whether neurolaw should be seen as a branch of neuroethics, the two have sufficiently distinct areas of inquiry to justify independent treatment. Gerben Meynen writes, "[Neurolaw] could be considered merely a branch of neuroethics, but that would not do justice to its central objective, which is examining the impact of neuroscience on the law" (2014: 819). What differentiates neurolaw is that, in general, it "deals in much more legal detail with the issues raised by neuroscience than is done in neuroethics." Whereas neuroethics might investigate ethical questions about the use of brain-based lie detection, neurolaw considers questions like: given the specific legal tests for admissibility of evidence in the United States, under what circumstances could brain-based lie detection be used in legal cases? Given its focus, then, on the meaning and implications of neuroscience for the law and legal practice, I maintain that whether or not neurolaw remains, in part, a branch of neuroethics, it is unique enough to deserve its own treatment.

1.2 Assessment, Intervention, and Revision

While there are different ways to go about classifying the different areas of neurolaw, I find it most helpful to divide them into three basic domains of investigation: assessment, intervention, and revision (Morse and Roskies 2013; Meynen 2014). The first domain, *assessment,* concerns evaluations of the state of mind/brain of individuals, including defendants, prisoners, and jurors. For instance, in the future, people's brains may be analyzed using neuroscientific techniques to answer questions about lying, insanity, risk of recidivism, or bias (Greely 2013; Meynen 2014). With respect to such assessments, "the reliability and validity of neuroscience technique, not just in research setting but specifically in criminal law cases, is a central topic of debate" (Meynen 2014: 820). It is in this domain that neurolaw investigates legal issues related to risk assessment for future violence, assessment of criminal responsibility or legal insanity, brain-based mind reading like evaluating biases in prospective jurors, and measuring deviant sexual appetites in defendants.

Consider, for instance, the mental state requirement in criminal cases and how it gave birth to forensic psychology and other methods of assessment.

In most cases, for a person to be convicted of a crime, the prosecutor must prove that the defendant committed an unlawful act (the *physical element*) and that they had the intention to commit the unlawful act (the *mental element*). The former is referred to as *actus reus*, the Latin phrase for "guilty act." Actus reus is the wrongful deed that comprises the physical component of a crime. In most criminal cases, actus reus must be coupled with *mens rea* – a "guilty mind" – for one to be held criminally liable. Mens rea represents the defendant's state of mind at the time of the crime, and the prosecution must prove that the defendant had the mental element of "guilty mind" while committing a crime to secure a conviction. There are, however, a number of *excuse defenses* that can be used to show that a defendant's mental state demonstrates that they should not be held legally responsible for a criminal act. Such excuses include insanity, diminished capacity, duress, mistake, and infancy.

Building on this, Nicole Vincent writes:

> [B]ecause of the increasing importance of this *mental element* in legal responsibility adjudication, with the passage of time, forensic psychiatrists have come to play an increasingly prominent role by helping courts to assess defendants' mental states, disorders, and mental capacities and by commenting on how these things might relate to legal criteria for responsibility. During this period, *medical* advances in the diagnosis and understanding of mental disorders were translated into increasingly more sophisticated *legal* tools for assessment and conceptualization of legal responsibility by gradually reshaping legal views about human agency. (2013: 2)

It is in this context that advances in the behavioral, cognitive, and neurosciences might again affect legal responsibility practices by "providing further insights into the nature of human agency and by offering revamped diagnostic criteria and more powerful diagnostic and intervention tools with which to assess and to alter minds" (Vincent 2013: 2–3). Neurolaw therefore seeks to investigate the potential benefits of using powerful new diagnostic brain imaging techniques to help assess the mental states, disorders, and mental capacities of defendants.

The second domain of neurolaw concerns all types of brain-based and law-related *interventions*. As Meynen explains, "In this domain, brains are not so much analyzed or interpreted, but changed" (2014: 821). In particular, he highlights three types of interventions: treatment, enhancement, and manipulation.

> Treatment (or restoration) may concern addicts in so-called drug courts: to what extent can or should they be coerced to follow treatment? The second type, enhancement, is discussed by Vincent [2014] who asks whether people's moral or legal responsibility, could be increased when their capacities would be significantly enhanced by neuroscientific interventions. The third type is manipulation. Brain-based interventions may also be deployed in

a perfidious way. People may find ways to make other people commit crimes. Can people who commit crimes because of brain-manipulation—for instance by deep brain stimulation—be held responsible for their actions? Is the law prepared for this kind of scenario? (2014: 821)

Each type of intervention raises its own unique issues. For instance, as our understanding of the brain increases, there has been growing support for neuroscientifically informed rehabilitation programs, which hold out the promise of reducing crime, increasing safety, and helping treat those offenders who suffer from mental health problems, addiction, pedophilic desires, and the like. These different types of interventions are made possible by new neuroscientific techniques and technologies – for example, transcranial magnetic stimulation, neurofeedback therapy, deep brain stimulation, and improved psychopharmaceuticals. But the opportunities they create – to treat, to enhance, and generally to modify people's minds – raise a number of vexing and important issues. For example, do such interventions violate the conditions for legally effective informed consent, alter an agent's personal identity in philosophically problematic ways, or otherwise violate an agent's rights? These are just some of the questions neurolaw investigates within the domain of intervention.

The third and final domain, *revision*, concerns the extent to which neuroscientific findings require us to revise, or even eliminate, parts of the law. Consider, for instance, the criminal prosecution of children. Currently, over half of the states in the United States still have no minimum age for prosecuting children, leaving eight-, nine-, and ten-year-old children vulnerable to extreme punishment, trauma, and abuse within adult jails and prisons. This has led to prosecutors across the country prosecuting young children in adult court. While the United States may be an outlier in the practice of prosecuting young children, it is by no means alone. Australian law also currently allows children as young as ten to be charged with a criminal offence, falling below the most common minimum age of criminal responsibility worldwide of 14. Children, however, are especially immature and impulsive and have not yet developed mature judgment or the ability to accurately assess risks and consequences. A neuroscientific understanding of adolescent brains could help us decide whether our current legal practices need to be revised (see Hirstein, Sifferd, and Fagan 2018).

Another area where revision is possible, though far more controversial, has to do with the law's assumptions about free will and moral responsibility and whether they can be reconciled with a neuroscientific understanding of human agency. Some theorists, for instance, maintain that neuroscience shows that free will is an illusion. Therefore, nobody is truly responsible for their actions, hence the criminal law has to be revised (Greene and Cohen 2004; Alces 2018). Others maintain that neuroscience is completely irrelevant to criminal law and, hence, no major revisions are necessary (Morse 2005, 2013, 2015, 2018). This aspect of neurolaw can be framed as a concrete instance of the challenge of fusing what Wilfrid Sellars called the *manifest* and *scientific images* of human beings. As Roth explains:

> Central to the manifest image is the conception of a human being as a *person*: a free, rational, responsible agent who makes choices and acts for reasons. By contrast, the conception of a human being delivered by the scientific image is that of a complex bio-chemical system whose behavior conforms to causal laws ... Attempts to bring neuroscience to bear on legal theory and practice will founder until we resolve this issue, for while neuroscience is situated within the scientific image, our legal system clearly has its home in the manifest image. (2018: 1)

While some neurolaw practitioners think a fusion of the manifest and scientific images is possible (Hirstein, Sifferd, and Fagan 2018; Roth 2018), others disagree (Greene and Cohen 2004; Alces 2018). For instance, Joshua Greene and Jonathan Cohen have famously argued that neuroscience will motivate us to re-examine criminal legal doctrines and penal policies that presuppose wrong-doers can be morally responsible for their actions in the desert-based sense:

> [N]euroscience will probably have a transformative effect on the law ... by transforming people's moral intuitions about free will and responsibility. This change in moral outlook will result ... from a new appreciation of old arguments, bolstered by vivid new illustrations provided by cognitive neuroscience. We foresee, and recommend, a shift away from punishment aimed at retribution in favor of a more progressive, consequentialist approach to the criminal law. (2004: 1775)

Whether or not they are correct about this is something I will explore further in Section 4, but note how the last sentence captures both the descriptive and normative aspects of what neurolaw aims to investigate – that is, Greene and Cohen make both a *prediction* about how neuroscience will impact the legal system as well as a *normative* endorsement for revision. Given that how things are (or will be in the future) can be distinct from how they *ought* to be, they can be right about one, both, or neither of these claims. Hence, neurolaw investigates both types of questions.

1.3 Metaphysical, Moral/Social, and Evidential Issues

In addition to the three domains of neurolaw just outlined, we can also say that within each, the kinds of issues that arise typically fall into one or more of the following categories: *metaphysical*, *moral/social*, and *evidential* (Roth 2018: 8). Foremost among the metaphysical issues relevant to neurolaw are the nature of human beings, the mind-body problem, and the question of free will (Roth 2018: 8). Consider, for instance, the case of Charles Whitman. By all accounts, Whitman was a smart, talented, and popular young man – a paradigm of the "all-American boy." He was an Eagle Scout, ex-marine, and promising engineering student. Yet on August 1, 1996, Whitman did the unthinkable. He killed his wife and mother and then went on a shooting spree at the University of Texas at Austin. He fatally shot three people inside UT Austin's Main Building and then ascended to twenty-eighth-floor observation deck on the building's clock tower. There, he fired at random people for ninety-six minutes. In the end, he killed sixteen people and wounded thirty-two others before being shot to death by police. Months early, however, Whitman began complaining of severe, persistent, and painful headaches. He also confessed in his journal of "being the victim of many unusual and irrational thoughts." In his suicide note, Whitman requested an autopsy be done to examine his brain since he was convinced it would show some "visible physical disorder." The autopsy confirmed Whitman's suspicions. It revealed a large tumor in Whitman's brain which had impacted the amygdala, a structure of the brain implicated in regulating emotions, including fear and aggression.

While Whitman's case is disturbing for a number of reasons, it is by no means unique. In fact, neuroscientists are beginning to shed new light on how brain lesions can lead to criminal behavior. A recent study conducted by Darby et al. (2017) systematically reviewed seventeen known cases where criminal behavior was preceded by the onset of a brain lesion. They found that while the lesions were distributed throughout different brain regions, all the lesions were part of the same functional network located on a single circuit that normally allows neurons throughout the brain to cooperate with each other on specific cognitive tasks. The network identified by the researchers is closely related to networks previously linked with moral decision-making. In particular, the network is most closely associated with two specific components of moral psychology: *theory of mind* and *value-based decision-making* (Darby et al. 2017). Theory of mind refers to the capacity to understand other people's points of view, beliefs, and emotions. This helps you appreciate, for instance, how your actions would make another person feel. Value-based decision-making refers to the ability to judge the value of specific actions or their outcomes. This helps you see not only what the outcome of your actions will be, but whether those actions and outcomes are good or bad.

Cases like Whitman's highlight just how important metaphysical questions are to the criminal law. Did Whitman's brain tumor make him go on a killing spree? If so, did he have the kind of control in action (i.e., free will) required for desert-based moral responsibility when he committed his crimes? More generally, as our predictive grasp of complex behavior improves, how will the bolstered sense that the mind is *identical* with, *supervenient* on, or *emergent* from the brain affect or undermine our notions of free will or moral responsibility? What if *everything* we do is the result of our neurobiology? And what if that neurobiology were the result of the same deterministic laws of nature that dictate the behavior of all other physical things in the physical universe? How we answer these questions will have a major impact on the kinds of issues investigated by neurolaw, especially with regard to the domain of revision.

These metaphysical questions also have direct relevance to neurolaw in connection with the second category of *moral/social* issues. The problem of free will, for instance, is intimately connected with our moral and legal practices and institutions. In fact, most contemporary philosophers simply define free will as the control in action required for a particular but pervasive sense of moral responsibility. This sense of moral responsibility is typically picked out by the notion of *basic desert* (see Pereboom 2001, 2014; Caruso and Morris 2017; Caruso 2021a; Caruso and Pereboom 2022). As Derk Pereboom defines it:

> For an agent to be morally responsible for an action in this sense is for it to be hers in such a way that she would deserve to be blamed if she understood that it was morally wrong, and she would deserve to be praised if she understood that it was morally exemplary. The desert at issue here is *basic* in the sense that the agent would deserve to be blamed or praised just because she has performed the action, given an understanding of its moral status, and not, for example, merely by virtue of consequentialist or contractualist considerations. (2014: 2)

Understood this way, free will is a kind of power or ability that an agent must possess in order to justify certain kinds of basically deserved attitudes, judgments, and treatments – such as resentment, indignation, moral anger, and retributive punishment. These reactions would be justified on purely backward-looking grounds; that's what makes them *basic* and would not appeal to consequentialist or forward-looking considerations such as future protection, future reconciliation, or future moral formation.

By defining free will as the control in action required for basic desert moral responsibility, it's easy to see the practical importance of the traditional debate to our moral and social lives. If it turns out, for instance, that agents lack the kind of free will required for basic desert moral responsibility, then *no one* is deserving of praise and blame in the basic sense (Pereboom 2001, 2014, 2021; Caruso 2021a).

Adopting this skeptical position would also undermine the retributive justification of legal punishment, since it does away with the idea of basic desert altogether – that is, if agents do not deserve blame just because they have knowingly done wrong, neither do they deserve punishment just because they have knowingly done wrong (Pereboom 2014: 157; Caruso 2021a). For this reason, neurolaw concerns itself not only with the moral/social/legal implications of the traditional free will debate, but also with the aims of our criminal justice system, including the practice of holding people criminally responsible and the underlying rationale for adopting the legal definitions and distinctions that inform judgments of legal responsibility.

The final category concerns *evidential* issues, such as the methods or procedures by which we come to *know* about the biological and psychological states of people (Roth 2018: 9). These issues most closely align with the domain of assessment, especially when brain scans are used to assess defendants and then introduced during court proceedings as, say, exculpatory evidence of brain damage or insanity. Here, we must ask: What do these brain images purport to show? How were they produced? And how reliable is the information provided by them?

> For neurolaw, the central concerns revolve around the instruments we use to gather evidence about brains and what we may or may not reasonably infer from such evidence . . . Achieving clarity here will require an examination of both the various technologies used to observe brains—including positron emission tomography (PET) and functional magnetic resonance imaging (fMRI)—and the underlying theoretical commitments that inform our interpretations of evidence and the inferences we make from such evidence. It will also require us to confront complications that arise for forensic neuroscience, or the attempts to use the tools of neuroscience to investigate crime. (Roth 2018: 9–10)

Neurolaw, therefore, investigates whether brain-based methods of assessment should be introduced in court proceedings and, if so, what evidential weight they should be given.

Bringing everything together, we can now say that the domains of assessment, intervention, and revision, together with the metaphysical, moral/social, and evidential issues addressed by neurolaw, yield the classification of neurolaw topics shown in Table 1:[2]

---

[2] I do not mean to suggest that this is the *only* way to classify the different domains, topics, and issues of neurolaw, nevertheless I think it provides a useful entry into the area of neurolaw and helps clarify its many different facets.

Table 1 Based on the table provided by Meynen (2014: 820), but with the addition of the third column and the inclusion of additional examples

Domain	Examples	Kinds of Issues
Assessment	• Determining competency, insanity, guilt, and sentencing • Risk assessment for future violence • Brain-based mind reading and lie detection	• Evidential • Moral/Social
Intervention – Treatment	• Addiction treatment • Chemical castration • Neurofeedback therapy • Deep brain stimulation, etc.	• Moral/Social
– Enhancement – Manipulation	• Cognitive and moral enhancement • Manipulating people to commit crimes • Manipulating people for their own, or society's, benefit	

Revision	• Insights from neuroscience may cause us to revise our attitudes about: free will and moral responsibility
	  ○ adolescent brains
	  ○ psychopathy
	  ○ insanity and other exculpatory conditions
		• Metaphysical
		• Moral/Social

2 Assessment

In 1974, Cecil Clayton was injured while working in a sawmill. A piece of wood broke off a log he was sawing and lodged in his brain. Surgery was required to remove the object, and this procedure resulted in the loss of nearly eight percent of Clayton's brain and 20 percent of his frontal lobe. Two months later, he checked himself into a mental hospital, frightened by his suddenly uncontrollable temper. Prior to the accident, Clayton had been an intelligent, guitar-playing family man. He abstained from alcohol, worked part time as a pastor, paid weekly visits to a local nursing home, and was a loving husband and father (Kaplan 2015). After the accident, everything changed. According to Clayton's brother Marvin, "He broke up with his wife, began drinking alcohol and became impatient, unable to work and more prone to violent outbursts" (*State* v. *Clayton* II, 63 S.W.3d at 204). Clayton spent the next twenty years trying to get psychiatric help, suffering from extreme depression, violent episodes, anxiety, and hallucinations.

But Clayton's spiraling mental state and increasingly violent behavior came to a head in 1996 when he shot and killed Christopher Castetter, a sheriff's deputy responding to a domestic disturbance between Clayton and his girlfriend.

During the guilt phase of his trial, Clayton's attorneys argued that "the effects of his 1972 accident left him blameless for the 1996 murder of Deputy Castetter and/or incompetent to proceed in some – but not all – stages of his case" (*State ex rel. Cecil Clayton* v. *Cindy Griffith*, SC94841). They claimed that the accident rendered him incapable of deliberating or forming the intent necessary for the jury to find him guilty of first-degree murder (*State* v. *Clayton* II, 63 S.W.3d at 204). Two experts testified that he was not capable of "deliberating, planning, or otherwise coolly reflecting on a murder when agitated" (*State* v. *Clayton* II, 63 S.W.3d at 204). The jury, however, rejected this evidence and found Clayton guilty of first-degree murder. In the penalty phase of his trial, Clayton argued that his brain injury was a mitigating factor that should make the death penalty inappropriate in his case (*State* v. *Clayton* II, 63 S.W.3d at 209–10). The jury rejected this as well and recommended that Clayton be sentenced to death.

Just prior to his execution, Clayton's defense team filed a petition asking for a stay of execution from the US Supreme Court. As evidence of Clayton's lack of competency and (full) responsibility, they submitted a scan of his brain showing a large area missing from his frontal lobe. They also provided evidence that he had an IQ of 71, which is considered borderline intellectually disabled. The petition argued that it would be unconstitutional to execute Clayton because under a series of rulings in recent years the US Supreme Court has banned judicial killings of insane and intellectually disabled people. The Supreme Court, however, rejected the petition and Clayton was executed via lethal injection in March 2015. His death, *The Washington Post* reported, "brought an end to nearly two decades of litigation during which it seemed that Clayton's brain, rather than the man himself, was on trial" (Kaplan 2015).

Cases like Cecil Clayton's raise a number of interesting questions about the use of neuroscientific data, such as brain scans, in assessing competency, insanity, guilt, and sentencing. As Xie, Berryessa, and Focquaert write: "For defendants like Clayton, for whom severe brain trauma appears to have influenced the exhibition of diminished moral reasoning, questions remain about what the 'correct' punishment or legal response should be" (2022: 2). According to Clayton's attorneys, he wasn't morally responsible for the shooting of Christopher Castetter – at least, not fully – since the damage to his brain "left him blameless." The court, of course, disagreed. But there have been other cases where similar defenses have helped defendants avoid the death penalty. In 2013, prison escapee and convicted murderer John McCluskey was sentenced to life without parole rather than death after his defense presented MRI evidence showing significant abnormalities in his frontal lobe. Arguments of this type, which maintain that a person's brain anatomy ought to change the way we assign guilt and punishment, have become increasingly common. In fact, cases where brain scans have been introduced as evidence have seen a marked upswing in the past few years (Denno 2015; Farahany 2016; Meixner 2016; Aono, Yaffe, and Kiber 2019).

In this section, I examine more closely brain-based *assessments* and the ethical issues associated with them. I begin by examining the use of neuroscientific evidence in the courtroom to determine competency, insanity, guilt, and sentencing. I then discuss how risk assessments are already being used to predict future violence and how neuropredictive technologies may one day be able to help improve existing assessments. I conclude by examining how courts of law might, in the future, replace current methods of lie detection with brain-based forms of mind reading and some of the potential concerns and questions associated with such technology.

2.1 Assessing Competency, Guilt, and Sentencing

From the introduction of the electroencephalograph (EEG) in the 1930s to the first magnetic resonance imaging (MRI) scans performed on humans in the 1970s, the twentieth century saw great advances in neuroscience and neuroimaging specifically. "These tools not only gave scientists an inside view into the structure and function of the human brain, but they also allowed experts to better conceptualize the connection between the human brain and human behavior" (Aono, Yaffe, and Kober 2019: 2). This connection has become particularly relevant in the courtroom since the more we understand about neuroscience, the more we see that even subtle abnormalities in the brain can affect moral reasoning and human behavior, which in turn can affect competency and blameworthiness. As a result, the use of neuroscientific evidence in criminal proceedings has increased significantly over the last two decades.

Francis Shen (2016) traces one of the earliest introductions of neuroscience into courtrooms to the 1940s when EEG was first used in a case involving a defendant with epilepsy. As new neuroimaging technologies emerged, they too made their way into the courtroom. In 1981, John Hinckley's attempted assassination of president Ronald Reagan led to one of the highest-profile cases that utilized neuroscience in a criminal trial. Hinckley's defense team introduced a computerized axial tomography (CAT) scan to help bolster their arguments that he suffered from schizophrenia due to a "shrunken" or atrophied brain and should therefore be found not guilty by reason of insanity. Although the prosecution opposed the introduction of Hinckley's CAT scans as evidence, arguing that it did not prove he had schizophrenia, it was ultimately allowed since the sort of brain atrophy he had was more common among schizophrenics than among the general population. Ultimately, the scans helped convince the jury, and they found Hinckley not responsible by reason of insanity (Aono, Yaffe, and Kober 2019: 2).

A decade later, a new form of neuroimaging made an appearance in *People v. Weinstein* (1992). Herbert Weinstein was charged with second-degree murder for strangling his wife and throwing her from the 12th floor of their Manhattan apartment, a charge he readily admitted to.

> His attorney's considered it suspicious that Weinstein would show little remorse for his actions and ordered positron emission tomography (PET) scans. At trial, Weinstein's defense team presented his PET scans to support their claim that, due to an arachnoid cyst, his brain function was disrupted. Thus, they claimed that the defendant did not have the requisite mental state to be found criminally responsible. (Aono, Yaffe, and Kober 2019: 2)

The arachnoid cyst was situated within the left sylvian fissure and compressed the left frontal, temporal, and insular regions of Weinstein's brain. Weinstein's attorney offered the PET scan in support of a claim of not guilty by reason of insanity. The prosecutor, on the other hand, moved to preclude any testimony or other evidence concerning the PET scan – arguing that PET scans were not accurate or reliable depictions of cerebral metabolism. While there was no doubt that the presence of the cyst altered Weinstein's brain structure and function, the question before the court was one of causation. As Susan Rushing writes: "Was there sufficient evidence to allow psychiatric and neurological experts to testify that Mr. Weinstein's brain abnormality was related to his violent criminal behavior?" (2014: 63). Unfortunately, we have no way of knowing how Weinstein's insanity claim would have fared before a jury because on the eve of trail he agreed to plead guilty to the lesser charge of manslaughter and was sentenced to seven to twenty-one years in prison.

In more recent decades, since around the turn of the century, the use of neuroscientific evidence in criminal trials has continued to increase (Farahany 2016; Meixner 2016). In a study of US cases between 2005 and 2012, Nita Farahany (2016) found that "the use of neurobiological evidence by criminal defendants is increasing year over year" (2016: 491). In particular, she found that 1585 judicial opinions from criminal cases discussed the use of neurobiological evidence by criminal defendants to bolster their criminal defense. In 2012 alone, there were 250 judicial opinions written in which the criminal defendant argued (successfully or otherwise) that their "brains made them do it" – more than double the number in 2007. In fact, Farahany found that 5 percent of all murder trials and 25 percent of all death penalty trials in 2012 featured criminal defendants making a bid for lower responsibility or lighter punishment using neurobiological data (2016: 486; see also Denno 2015).

Farahany's study also revealed additional surprising results and trends. While many scholars have discussed the implications of using neurobiological evidence for mitigating criminal punishment, Farahany found that the second most common use of neurobiological evidence in criminal cases is to challenge competency. She also found that the quality, and not just the quantity, of opinions discussing neurobiological evidence has evolved. Opinions earlier in the study often discussed neurobiological evidence as part of a laundry list of other types of scientific evidence introduced. In later opinions, however, "judges spilled substantial ink discussing the neurobiological evidence often in significant detail and with citations to scientific literature and the experts who testified in the case" (2016: 492). According to Farahany, this suggests "a shift in both the frequency and the nature of how such evidence is being evaluated by judges and juries in criminal cases" (2016: 492).

Despite this shift, important questions and criticisms remain. Critics, for instance, point out that the use of neurobiological evidence has thus far been rather "haphazard, ad hoc, and often illconceived" (Farahany 2016: 488–9). This is because, despite the caution and nuance neuroscientists typically advise, prosecutors and defense attorneys are often quick to introduce neurobiological evidence and sometimes even overstate it whenever they think it can help their case. Defense attorneys introduce neuroscientific evidence in attempts to exculpate criminal defendants, to bolster preexisting legal defenses, and to mitigate defendants' culpability and punishment. Prosecutors, on the other hand, have "seized upon the double-edge potential of a claimed neurobiological evidence to denigrate defendants' characters and to demonstrate defendants' likely future dangerousness" (Farahany 2016: 489). Given the gravity of such decisions, including assessments bearing on deservingness for capital punishment, it is important that we separate the wheat from the chaff and investigate the proper role of neuroscience in criminal proceedings.

While the interconnection between neuroscience and law is promising and rapidly developing, there are several critical methodological cautions we need to keep in mind. First, studies of how an average brain works do not always provide reliable information on how a specific individual's brain works. Functional imaging research typically relies on results based on population-level inferences, yet group average results may belie the unique patterns of activity present in the individual. Second, "there are many types of brain imaging techniques, with many accompanying ways to be interpreted and presented" (Du 2020: 511). For example, PET scans use radioactive tracers to detect blood concentrations in different brain regions that are associated with brain functions. EEGs record electrical activity in the brain, which is then analyzed with the aid of a computer system to allow for inferences about brain function. And functional MRI detects changes in hemodynamic properties of the brain that typically occur when engaging in particular mental tasks. As Yu Du writes: "It is vital to bear in mind that brain images are the result of a process within a process. In other words, many decisions and steps are involved in determining exactly when and what data should be collected and how the data should be analyzed and presented. The room for technical and statistical mistakes and misinterpretations can be significant" (2020: 512).

Another concern is that the meaning of brain images is not straightforward or self-evident. As such, inferring the psychological, moral, and/or legal significance of such images is not easy. We cannot detect mens rea or moral responsibility on a brain scan. "Even well-designed, well-executed, properly analyzed, and properly presented brain images must be interpreted in the correct context" (Du 2020: 513). Furthermore, identifying structural abnormalities in the brain and correlating them with violent behaviors is "complicated and subject to enormous variation" (Du 2020: 513). This is because "many brain regions are involved in a wide variety of functions" (Du 2020: 513). Additionally, the same task can also be accomplished in the presence of widely varying brain activation patterns. To make matters worse, *even when* a strong correlation can be established, it's generally not enough to prove causation. Nor is it always clear what it can tell us about competency, intent, and the state of mind of the individual at the time of the crime. It's possible, for instance, for neuroimaging to confirm that structural changes have occurred in the brain (due, say, to a brain injury or tumor) and perhaps even that this resulted in behavioral change. What it cannot do – and, hence, what is left for neurolaw practitioners to debate – is determine whether such functional and behavioral changes should reduce culpability or mitigate punishment. In some cases, it can be rather difficult to determine how much weight we should give to the neurobiological evidence and what, if anything, it can tell us about an individual's competency, guilt, and/or punishment.

I believe it's important, then, that when discussing the use of neuroscientific evidence, we keep all these methodological limitations in mind. Acknowledging these limitations, however, does not mean we should prohibit the use of neuroscience in court. To do so would be to throw the baby out with the bathwater. I contend that when used responsibly, neuroscientific evidence has the potential to improve the accuracy and decrease errors in the criminal justice system. I therefore agree with Farahany when she writes, "decrying the use of neurobiological evidence in criminal law seems both futile and counterproductive; neuroscience is already entrenched in the US legal system. And used appropriately, it holds promise of improving decision-making in law. An outright ban is neither warranted nor productive" (2016: 488). Rather than resisting this shift, then, neuroscientists should play a part in safeguarding these developments by helping educate the public and legal professionals about the responsible use of neuroscience in the courtroom.

One area where brain scans and neuroscientific evidence may be of value is in cases where a tumor or traumatic brain injury caused damage that resulted in a significant personality change. Here, "the role of neuroimaging is important to the case as it can provide evidence for a reason behind the alteration of their personality" (Straiton and Lake 2021: 70). Alteration in personality due to a structural change in the brain can include increased impulsiveness, depression, aggression, inappropriate sexual behavior, lack of thought control, and violence. Consider, for instance, the widely discussed case of a forty-year-old schoolteacher who experienced new-onset pedophilia due to a right orbitofrontal brain tumor – not once, but twice.

According to Jeffrey Burns and Russell Swerdlow (2003), the two neurologists who first treated the man, his behavior changed significantly in the year 2000. While the individual had a preexisting interest in pornography, he increasingly began to frequent Internet pornography sites that "emphasized children and adolescents and was specifically targeted to purveyors of child pornography" (2003: 437). The man also began soliciting prostitution at "massage parlors," which he had not previously done.

> The patient went to great lengths to conceal his activities because he felt that they were unacceptable. However, he continued to act on his sexual impulses, stating that "the pleasure principle overrode" his urge restraint. He began making subtle sexual advances toward his prepubescent stepdaughter, which he was able to conceal from his wife for several weeks. Only after the stepdaughter informed the wife of the patient's behavior did she discover with further investigation his emerging preoccupation with pornography, and child pornography in particular. The patient was legally removed from the home, diagnosed as having pedophilia, and prescribed medroxyprogesterone. He was found guilty of child molestation and was ordered by a judge to either undergo inpatient rehabilitation in a 12-step program for sexual addiction or go to jail. Despite his strong desire to avoid prison, he could not restrain himself from soliciting sexual favors from staff and other clients at the rehabilitation center and was expelled. (Burns and Swerdlow 2003: 437)

As a result, the judge sentenced him to prison. However, the night before entering prison, the man complained of severe headaches and was taken to the emergency room where, following an fMRI scan, it was revealed that he had a right orbitofrontal tumor. The tumor was removed, his behavior returned to normal, and he was deemed safe to go home to his wife and stepdaughter. Several months later, the sexually charged behavior returned, and it was discovered that the tumor had regrown. It was again removed, and once again his behavior returned to normal.

Since the man's symptoms were resolved each time the orbitofrontal hemangiopericytoma was removed, it seems reasonable to infer a causal connection between the man's behavioral changes and orbitofrontal disruption in his brain.

In fact, the two neurologists on the case themselves see this as "further establishing causality" (Burns and Swerdlow 2003: 439). According to them, the orbitofrontal disruption likely exacerbated a preexisting interest in pornography, manifesting as sexual deviancy and pedophilia. To their knowledge, "this is the first description of pedophilia as a specific manifestation of orbitofrontal syndrome" (2003: 439). They also go on to conclude that: "Our patient could not refrain from acting on his pedophilia despite the awareness that his behavior was inappropriate" (2003: 440). This conclusion, they claim, is supported both by the details of the case and the fact that "Orbitofrontal lesion research suggests that sociopathic behavior results from a loss of impulse control rather than a loss of moral knowledge" (2003: 439). In their professional opinion, the tumor interrupted connections between the orbitofrontal lobe and the amygdala – the region of the brain responsible for emotion and decision-making – therefore resulting in diminished impulse control.

This assessment seems to fit with everything we currently know about the orbitofrontal cortex. In fact, the orbitofrontal cortex is one region that has been consistently associated with antisocial or violent behavior, along with the anterior cingulate cortex and the dorsolateral prefrontal cortex – both also located in the frontal lobe (Yang and Raine 2009; Sajous-Turner et al. 2020; Straiton and Lake 2021). Neuroimaging studies have also found that patients who suffered injury to these regions of the prefrontal cortex show reduced decision-making capabilities and psychopathic-like behavior (Blair and Cipolotti 2000; Straiton and Lake 2021). Such research not only supports the neurologists' assessment in the new-onset pedophilia case, but it also highlights how neuroscience can be used in court to show how brain lesions and injuries – particularly ones to the frontal lobe – can radically reduce the ability to make rational decisions and check impulses.

Another area where neuroscientific evidence can be helpful is in determining punishment, especially in death penalty cases. On a case-by-case basis, there is unfortunately no hard and fast principle for determining when and to what extent neuroscientific evidence should lead a jury to a non-guilty verdict. As a result, in many cases, judges and juries may not find neuroscientific evidence convincing enough to completely absolve a defendant. However, if the guilty verdict is finalized and the decision is between a life sentence and the death penalty, neuroscientific evidence (along with other evidence about the impact of early life experiences, genetics, and epigenetics) could be relevant (Du 2020: 501).

During the penalty phase of capital trials, defendants may introduce mitigating evidence that argues for punishment less than death. Brain scans, for instance, can be used to identify and support defendants' claims of diminished culpability due to circumstances beyond their control in capital cases (Focquart, Glenn, and Raine 2013). Defendants may also introduce neuroscientific evidence of brain damage or dysfunctionality in an attempt to mitigate punishment. In fact, empirical research has shown that scientific evidence about a hypothetical defendant's brain function is likely to limit a sentence's severity. A study conducted in *Science* by Aspinwall, Brown, and Tabery (2012) found that, on average, judges subtracted a year from an imaginary convict's sentence after being told he was genetically predisposed to violence. And Edith Greene and Brain Cahill (2012) conducted a study assessing the impact of neuroscientific evidence on mock jurors' sentencing recommendations and impressions of a capital defendant. Using actual case facts, they manipulated diagnostic evidence presented by the defense (psychosis diagnosis, neuropsychological test results, and neuroimages) and found that defendants were less likely to be sentenced to death when jurors had this evidence than when they did not. They also found that neuropsychological and neuroimaging evidence had mitigating effects on impressions of the defendant.

While some theorists claim that neuroscientific evidence is a "double-edged sword" – one that will either get defendants completely off the hook or unfairly brand them as posing a future danger to society – a recent empirical analysis by Deborah Denno (2015) reveals this to be a myth. Her study evaluated 800 criminal cases involving neuroscientific evidence over the past two decades. It was the first to empirically and systematically investigate how courts assess the mitigating and aggravating strength of such evidence. Her analysis found, first, that neuroscientific evidence is "usually offered to mitigate punishments in the way that traditional criminal law has always allowed, especially in the penalty phase of death penalty trials" (2015: 493). Contrary to the popular image of neuroscience as a double-edged sword, her study found that "neuroscience evidence is typically introduced for a well-established legal purpose – to provide fact finders with more complete, reliable, and precise information when determining a defendant's fate" (2015: 493). Second, her study also found that "courts accept neuroscience evidence for this purpose, and in fact expect attorneys to raise this evidence when possible on behalf of their clients" (2015: 494). In fact, this expectation is so entrenched that "courts are willing to grant defendants their 'ineffective assistance of counsel' claims when attorneys fail to pursue this mitigating evidence" (2015: 495). Denno's study also found that "the potential future danger posed by defendants is rarely a facet of cases involving neuroscience evidence – again contradicting the myth of the double-edged sword" (2015: 495). Lastly, her study found that neuroscience evidence usually mitigates punishment, particularly for death penalty sentences. It seems, then, that neuroscientific evidence may be more influential at the sentencing phase than the liability (guilt or innocence) phase and is more likely to mitigate punishment than exacerbate it.

Instead, then, of entirely preventing the use of neuroscience in the courtroom to assess competency, guilt, and sentencing, I contend that its application should be careful, specialized, and context-specific. We must begin by acknowledging the methodological limitations outlined previously, including concerns about statistical significance, effect size, and the difficulty of making legal and psychological inferences. We must also acknowledge that the application of neuroscience in the courtroom is highly context-specific. That said, neuroscientific evidence is valuable "not because it creates something new but instead because it explains the normative behaviors and folk-psychological concepts within the legally relevant domain" (Du 2020: 515). When properly used, neuroscience can help us make more scientifically informed decisions within the courtroom by providing more complete, reliable, and precise information for already well-established legal purposes. We just need to be careful not to overplay the neuroscientific evidence. We must also demand that when brain scans are introduced into the courtroom, they are obtained, analyzed, interpreted, and presented by qualified experts. In short, neuroscience is a vital tool in making decisions about competency, guilt, and sentencing, but it must be used properly to ensure fairness.

2.2 Neurobiologically Informed Risk Assessment

I turn now to a discussion of neurobiologically informed risk assessment methods. Decisions about public safety and the prevention of violence are more likely to succeed when they are based on accurate predictions of who will engage in violence and under what circumstances. The problem, however, is that accurately predicting violence before it occurs is not easy. As Eyal Aharoni et al. explain:

> The criminal justice system has a problem: it is tasked with protecting society from dangerous offenders, but it cannot reliably predict who will and who will not reoffend. Given that its predictions are imperfect, efforts to deter or incapacitate dangerous offenders will sometimes encroach on the rights of non-dangerous individuals, and conversely, efforts to protect the non-dangerous will sometimes harbor some "bad apples." To the extent that predictive errors can be reduced, our society could become safer and more just. (2022: 161)

One potential way to reduce predictive error is to develop better risk assessment tools. Traditionally, offender risk estimates were determined using unstructured clinical judgment by trained forensic psychologists – a subjective technique that has since been shown to perform little better than chance. Recently, structured actuarial risk assessment techniques have improved the accuracy of offender placement decisions by quantifying the offender's degree of fit with a known validation sample. As a result, more than twenty US states now require their courts to use these statistical tools in service of offender sentencing and placement decisions (Aharoni et al. 2022: 161–62).

In the criminal justice context, *structured actuarial risk assessment* refers to any evidence-based technique that generates probabilistic predictions about the ostensible offender's engaging in certain behavior (e.g., violence, reoffending, relapsing, or responding to treatment) by querying information about their attributes or circumstances (Taxman 2018; Aharoni et al. 2022: 161–62). Before we discuss the pros and cons of common risk assessment techniques, it is important to understand the variety of ways in which these techniques can be, and often are, employed in legal settings. Aharoni et al. (2022: 163) provide the following very useful list:

- After a person is arrested, risk information might be useful to prosecutors making charging decisions. Prosecutors have wide discretion in such decisions. So, if a defendant is perceived to be particularly dangerous, a prosecutor might seek to file more charges or more severe charges.
- Bail decisions may also be informed by risk information.
- Risk assessments can also inform whether the individual is placed on probation or instead sentenced to prison. Risk scores are not typically used to influence the *length* of a prison sentence, but may be used in pre-sentencing reports and could be considered relevant to actual sentencing decisions—for example, in Texas, capital sentencing hinges in part on a determination of future dangerousness (Tex. Code Crim. Proc., Art. 37.071).
- Within a facility, risk information can determine security level assignments: Authorities may assign low, medium, or high supervision based on the offender's recent behavior in custody, not as punishment but as a protective measure.
- A prison inmate could be released to parole prior to his sentence end date on grounds of a low risk assessment score.
- Treatment interventions can be based on risk assessment. In some states, such as Florida, judges can mandate treatments such as anti-androgen therapy (i.e., "chemical castration") to certain sex offenders in addition to their original sentence based on their risk of reoffending (Fla. § 794.0235). Risk assessment can also inform decisions to administer treatment (typically noninvasive treatment) as a sentencing diversion.

In addition to these uses, risk assessment tools also lie at the heart of criminal justice reform to tackle mass incarceration. Melissa Hamilton, for instance, writes, "The newest application of risk tools centers on the pretrial stage as a means to reduce both reliance upon wealth-based bail systems and rates of pretrial detention" (2021a: 53).

This is an extremely important issue since three out of five people in US jails today have not been convicted of a crime. This amounts to nearly half a million people sitting in jail each day, despite being presumed innocent under the law. The vast majority of these individuals are awaiting trial but cannot afford the bail amount set for pretrial release. While the use of cash bail is ubiquitous in the United States, it is also fundamentally unjust (Caruso 2020b). The cash bail system criminalizes poverty, as people who are unable to afford bail are detained while they await trial. In this way, cash bail perpetuates inequities in the justice system that are disproportionately felt by black and brown communities and those experiencing poverty. Furthermore, the legal rationale for pretrial detention is public safety. Yet the ability to pay cash bail is neither an indicator of a person's guilt nor an indicator of risk in release. In fact, the cash bail system often leads to the detention of people who pose no real threat to public safety (Laura and John Arnold Foundation 2013).

Despite its many potential advantages, critics fear that risk assessment tools may lead to negative consequences if they do not exhibit sufficient accurate predictions or do not treat protected groups fairly. One key concern is that current risk assessment tools tend to be algorithmic. They use big data and statistical analyses to derive correlates of criminal offending and package them into computational algorithms (Taxman 2018; Hamilton 2021a, 2021b). If the data being used is already biased because of, say, the over policing of black and brown communities or historical biases elsewhere in the legal system, then the predictions produced by these tools will simply reflect and reinforce existing cultural biases. For this reason, the potential for race-based discrimination is an emerging concern regarding the use of algorithmic risk assessment methods (Hamilton 2021a, 2021b). Critics fear that black defendants may be harmed when the algorithms learn on already biased data, imbed these structural inequalities, and further relaunder inequities through the guise of objective risk prediction.

This concern is a serious one, and we must do everything we can to guard against the possibility of algorithmic bias. That said, I also think it would be a mistake to completely abandon or prohibit the use of structured actuarial risk assessments over such concerns. For one, it's possible that once we recognize the existence of such algorithmic bias, we can design better tools that avoid it. The first step is to recognize that such biases exist and that historic incarceration data may overestimate the risk of offending in certain populations. Once we recognize this, we can work to create more accurate and less biased tools for assessing risk – for example, tools that focus less on demographic factors, which may be more susceptible to bias, and more on factors unique to the individual, such as substance use problems, psychopathic personality features, anger, impulsivity, antisocial peers, antisocial attitudes, a history of violence, young age at the first violent act, stress, treatment nonadherence, lack of social support, and mental illness. Second, we have to weigh the use of structured actuarial risk assessment tools against the alternative – the status quo. I'll argue in a moment that when we do this, we see that such tools, while not perfect, are a marked improvement over traditional methods of judging risk and dangerousness. Lastly, in the near future, neuropredictive technologies may allow us to further reduce bias by including unique neurobiological markers in our risk assessments.

Scientists, for instance, are beginning to examine "whether the inclusion of neurobiological and/or genetic markers can improve predictive models based solely on non-biological evidence" (Aharoni et al. 2022: 168). In fact, a growing number of theorists have suggested that in the near future, *neuropredictive technologies* may be able to further improve our risk assessment methods, both in terms of accuracy and counterbalancing human bias (Nadelhoffer et al. 2012; Aharoni et al. 2022). Neuroscientists, for instance, have made tremendous progress in the past two decades in identifying and exploring some of the neural correlates of violence and aggression (Raine 2014).

Consider, as an example, what neuroscientists have learned about the brains of individuals with psychopathy, a developmental disorder that often leads to persistent antisocial behavior. Despite the fact that only 1 percent or less of the population is thought to be afflicted with psychopathy, some estimates suggest that individuals with psychopathy could nevertheless be responsible for as much as 30–40 percent of all violent crime (Hare and McPherson 1984). Psychopaths are particularly prone to violence demonstrating increased aggressive behavior and committing a great number of violent attacks than nonpsychopaths (Salekin et al. 1996). Psychopathy is also a strong predictor of how likely one is to re-offend after release from prison (Porter et al. 2001), and it is a particularly strong predictor of violent recidivism (Cornell et al. 1996; Porter et al. 2009). In fact, within one year of release psychopaths are about three times more likely to recidivate than non-psychopaths, and four times more likely to violently recidivate (Hemphill et al. 1998).

Over the last few decades, neuroscientists have begun to study the neuronal basis of psychopathy (see Raine et al. 2000; Glenn et al. 2010; Glenn, Yang, and Raine 2012). Leutgeb et al. (2015), for example, compared structural imaging data from forty male high-risk violent offenders and thirty-seven nondelinquent healthy controls via voxel-based morphometry – a computational approach to neuroanatomy that measures differences in local concentrations of brain tissue. They then correlated psychopathic traits and risk for violence recidivism with gray matter volume of regions previously shown relevant for criminal behavior. They found that (a) relative to controls, criminals showed less gray matter volume in the prefrontal cortex and more gray matter volume in cerebellar regions and basal ganglia structures; (b) within criminals, there was a negative correlation between prefrontal gray matter volume and psychopathy; (c) there was a positive correlation between cerebellar gray matter volume and psychopathy as well as risk of recidivism for violence; (d) gray matter volumes of the basal ganglia and supplementary motor area were positively correlated with antisociality, and (e) that gray matter volume of the amygdala was negatively correlated with risk for violence recidivism. They concluded that in violent offenders, deviations in gray matter volume of the prefrontal cortex as well as areas involved in the motor component of impulse control (cerebellum, basal ganglia, supplementary motor area) are differentially related to psychopathic traits and the risk of violence recidivism. Other neuroimaging investigations have found reductions in orbitofrontal gray matter in psychopaths as well as volume reduction in the most anterior frontopolar regions of the prefrontal cortex (de Oliveira-Souza et al. 2008; Tiihonen et al. 2008).

The amygdala also features prominently in theories of psychopathy due to its role in forming stimulus-reinforcement associations, conditioned fear responses, and the initiation of affective states. Recent neuroimaging data have strongly implicated the involvement of the amygdala in psychopathy-related deficits (Anderson and Kiehl 2014). In one large-scale investigation involving nearly 300 incarcerated subjects, Ermer et al. (2011) found that psychopathy was associated with decreased regional gray matter in several paralimbic and limbic areas, including the amygdala. Yang et al. (2010) also found that volume reductions in both the prefrontal cortex and the amygdala were more pronounced in psychopaths with criminal convictions compared to both controls and "successful" psychopaths. Given these new insights into the neurological correlates of psychopathy, neuroscientific methods may have the potential to improve existing tools for predicting violent recidivism (Leutgeb et al. 2015: 194).

Beyond psychopathy, it's also possible that we may be able to improve predictions of antisocial behavior more generally by including targeted brain metrics in risk assessment models. For instance, in a series of studies conducted by Aharoni et al. (2013), they found that in a sample of ninety-six adult offenders who engaged in an impulse control task while undergoing functional magnetic resonance imaging, brain activity within the *anterior cingulate cortex* (ACC) prospectively predicted being rearrested later. Offenders with relatively low ACC activity had roughly double the odds of getting rearrested for a violent or nonviolent crime as those with high activity, controlling for other known risk factors. In fact, using advanced statistical techniques, these neuropredictive models demonstrated relatively high accuracy – that is, the probability that a true positive was correctly classified exceeded 75 percent (Aharoni et al. 2014). Other studies have reported similar predictive effects using different models of brain function (Kiehl et al. 2018; Delfin et al. 2019). Together, "these studies provide preliminary evidence that brain factors such as ACC function may serve as candidate biomarkers for antisocial behavior" (Aharoni et al. 2022: 170). Perhaps in the future, then, we will be able to additionally improve existing actuarial risk assessment tools by incorporating neuropredictive technologies, further increasing their accuracy and reducing subjective bias.

Despite these advances in actuarial risk assessment, its use in legal settings continues to be the subject of much scholarly debate. Many ethicists, for instance, suggest that "all actuarial risk assessment is too problematic for use in justice settings, cautioning about violations of beneficence (e.g., unjustified harm to offenders), justice (e.g., unfair distribution of sanctions), and respect for persons (e.g., unjustified restrictions on the offender's freedom or exposure to his private mental life), among other problems" (Aharoni et al. 2022: 162). Such opposition, however, needs to be considered in contrast with its alternative: the status quo. Aharoni et al. (2022) examine such ethical concerns and argue that:

> ... while some uses of actuarial risk assessment might potentially violate individual rights to beneficence, justice, and respect for persons, these problems arise not just for evidence-based tools but for any decision procedure that society adopts to protect the public safety and civil rights of its members by trying to identify potentially dangerous individuals. We therefore attempt to shift the debate from *whether* actuarial risk assessment is justified to *when* ... We argue that appeals to individual rights alone are not sufficient to distinguish between ethically appropriate and inappropriate application of actuarial risk assessment. Any principled attempt to evaluate the appropriateness of risk tools must, *for each application*, evaluate its unique coasts *relative* to its benefits and *relative* to traditional clinical approaches (i.e., the status quo). (2022: 162)

I agree with Aharoni et al. that, when applied to various uses by the law, actuarial risk assessment often *fares better* on key ethical criteria than traditional clinical methods.

One common concern critics raise is that the predictive accuracy of actuarial risk assessments is insufficient for widespread use. This concern, however, is misleading since meta-analysis has demonstrated that the predictive value of many actuarial risk assessment instruments is superior to the traditional methods that would otherwise be used (Grove and Meehl 1996). Traditional risk assessment techniques rely heavily on unstructured clinical judgments to assess the risk of antisocial behavior. Given that clinical assessment is inherently subjective, "it is unsurprising that the resulting predictions of future dangerousness are so unreliable" (Aharoni et al. 2022: 164). In fact, "some commentators have even gone so far as to suggest that relying on clinical risk assessment for the purposes of the law is tantamount to 'flipping coins in the courtroom'" (Aharoni et al. 2022: 164). Worse still, "the unguided and intuitive nature of the process also makes it possible for biases and prejudices of clinicians to influence their assessments." It's my view, then, that while we should continue to strive to increase the power of actuarial risk assessment, it already represents a significant step forward, "even if it falls short of some critics' idealized standards" (Aharoni et al. 2022: 171).

Another main class of concerns critics raise has to do with potential violations of norms of beneficence, justice, and respect for persons. For example, "false-positive errors could support a longer sentence or revocation of privileges from a non-dangerous offender, and false-negative errors could result in an early release of a dangerous offender, placing the community members at risk of victimization" (Aharoni et al. 2022: 173). To avoid these errors, one may be tempted to prohibit the use of actuarial risk assessment in an effort to minimize unnecessary harm. Unfortunately:

> ... removing risk assessment does not reduce harm. Judges are obligated to make sanctioning decisions with consideration for public safety regardless of whether an actuarial risk assessment is employed. The only other alternative (clinical judgment) still yields classification errors that are likely to be substantially larger without actuarial risk assessment than with it ... So, revocation of actuarial risk assessment on grounds of its harmfulness perversely increases harm by increasing the number of low-risk offenders who will be needlessly sanctioned and also the number of community members who will become victims of a truly dangerous person who was misclassified. (Aharoni et al. 2022: 173)

The central point here is that if we remove all actuarial risk assessments, violations of beneficence, justice, and respect for persons will not simply go away. Instead, they may actually *increase* since the alternative yields even greater classification errors.

The question, then, should not be whether the use of risk judgments is without serious and important moral concerns, but whether the use of *particular actuarial risk factors* is any more problematic than the other alternatives (Nadelhoffer et al. 2012; Douglas et al. 2017; Aharoni et al. 2022). I contend that in many cases it may actually be less problematic. This is not to advocate, of course, for the uncritical use of actuarial risk assessment. Instead, the justification of such assessments must be judged relative to the ways in which they are to be used and what the other alternative options are. Of course, for these tools to be effective and ethical, developers need to continue to work on minimizing bias and increasing accuracy. But here too actuarial risk assessment may have an advantage over traditional methods: "By design, actuarial risk assessment attempts to codify risk factors. This feature makes the process transparent and enables us to monitor and evaluate procedural mistakes and ultimately to minimize bias" (Aharoni et al. 2022: 178). For this reason, risk assessment tools enable the assumptions of the predictive models to be explicit and subject to evaluation and revision. This level of transparency is not found in traditional clinical methods. As a result, if we dispense with structured actuarial risk assessment in justice decisions, "assessment bias does not go away, it just exerts its nasty effects behind a curtain of opacity" (Aharoni et al. 2022: 179).

Moving forward, then, I suggest that the results of independent research can productively inform policymakers and stakeholders who are interested in ensuring the utility and fairness of the assessment instruments they may employ. The use of risk assessment is ubiquitous in our legal system. Since the use of risk assessment is not likely going away, we should continue to study and evaluate different actuarial risk assessment instruments, adopting those with the highest rate of predictive accuracy and the lowest rate of bias. We should also continue to work on ways to improve our existing assessment methods, which could include adding neurobiological measures to characterize biological markers of human behavior that increase the ability to predict particular behavioral outcomes accurately. A good test for whether we should do this would be whether explanations of human behaviors demonstrate greater predictive accuracy when the relevant biological, neural, psychological, and social factors are all included in the model (Aharoni et al. 2022: 169).

2.3 Mind Reading and Lie Detection

I turn now to another controversial topic in the domain of assessment: the use of neuroimaging techniques in "mind reading" and lie detection. Traditional lie detection tools, such as polygraph, voice stress analysis, or special interrogation techniques, rely on behavior or psychophysiological manifestations of deception. With the advent of neuroimaging techniques, "the question emerged whether it would be possible to directly identify deceit in the part of the body where it is generated: the brain" (Gamer 2014: 172). After a few promising studies, these techniques became commercially available, and there have been attempts to use such results in court – though such attempts have thus far been unsuccessful. In this section, I will briefly review the development of neuroimaging techniques in the field of deception detection and critically discuss the potential benefits and shortcomings of such methods. I will also discuss some of the moral and legal issues associated with such technologies, such as concerns over rights and privacy.

Within the law, a reliable and valid detection of deception is of significant interest and has attracted a substantial amount of research during the last few decades. As Matthias Gamer writes, "From an applied perspective, such [a] method should be easy to handle, applicable to individual cases, resistant to countermeasures, and yield accurate diagnoses" (2014: 172). When polygraphy was first introduced, it promised to provide just such a method and was widely adopted by investigative authorities all over the world. A polygraph is a device or procedure that measures and records several physiological indicators such as blood pressure, pulse, respiration, and skin conductivity while a person is asked and answers a series of questions. The theory underpinning the use of the polygraph is that deceptive answers will produce physiological responses that can be differentiated from those associated with nondeceptive answers. However, while polygraphs are sometimes used as an interrogation tool with criminal suspects or candidates for sensitive public or private sector employment, they have questionable reliability and, as a result, are generally not admissible as evidence in court. In fact, assessments of polygraphy by scientific and government bodies generally suggest that polygraphs are highly inaccurate, may easily be defeated by countermeasures, and are an imperfect or invalid means of assessing truthfulness (US Congress Office of Technology Assessment 1983; American Psychological Association 2004; Gamer 2014).

One promising new method makes use of neuroimaging techniques, which have opened the way for a new and different approach to detecting deception. The key idea is that by examining the brain directly, we can hopefully find "a specific signature of deception in the brain activity that would allow for a sensitive and accurate detection of deceit" (Gamer 2014: 173). One advantage of using neuroimaging techniques is that brain activity can be noninvasively measured in humans, either by recording cortical electric activity from the scalp using electroencephalography or by measuring neurovascular changes with Positron Emission Tomography (PET) or functional magnetic resonance imaging (fMRI).

One of the first studies to use functional magnetic resonance imaging (fMRI) to detect deception at the individual level was conducted by Kozel and colleagues (2005). In the study, subjects participated in a mock crime and were instructed to either steal a ring or a watch from a drawer. Kozel et al. then used fMRI to show that specific regions were reproducibly activated when subjects deceived. While undergoing fMRI, subjects were asked questions about both objects (e.g., "Did you steal the watch?" "Did you take the ring from the drawer?") and instructed to deny stealing anything. As participants were familiar with both objects and delivered the same response ("No"), these questions only differ with respect to truthful or deceptive responding. In the study, a Model-Building Group (MBG, n = 30) was used to develop the analysis methods, and the methods were subsequently applied to an independent Model-Testing Group (MTG, n = 31). Kozel et al. (2005) were able to correctly differentiate truthful from deceptive responses, correctly identifying the object stolen, for 93 percent of the subjects in the MBG and 90 percent of the subjects in the MTG.

Comparable results were observed in other studies that used different statistical procedures (see, e.g., Davatzikos et al. 2005; Ganis et al. 2011). For instance, Davatzikos et al. (2005) used a multivariate nonlinear high-dimensionality pattern classification method applied to fMRI images to discriminate between the spatial patterns of brain activity associated with lying and truth. In the study, twenty-two participants were presented with an envelope containing two cards (five clubs and seven spades). In the imaging phase of the study, the investigator instructed participants to deny possession of one of the cards and acknowledge possession of the other. Davatzikos and colleagues were able to correctly discriminate 99 percent of the true and false responses. These results, Davatzikos et al. conclude, "demonstrate the potential of non-linear machine learning techniques in lie detection and other possible clinical applications of fMRI in individual subjects, and indicate the accurate clinical tests could be based on measurements of brain function with fMRI" (2005: 663).

While these results look promising, we are still a long way off from reliable neuroimaging-based lie detection. For a deception detection method to be trustworthy, not only must it be applicable to individual cases and yield accurate diagnoses, but it must also be resistant to countermeasures. However, Ganis et al. (2011) tested whether countermeasures – methods prevaricators employ to confuse deception detection procedures – could defeat fMRI deception tests. Using a modified concealed information test (CIT) in which participants lied about knowing their birth date when shown six dates on a computer, Ganis et al. (2011) instructed some participants how to perform a countermeasure consisting in associating distinct covert actions to the irrelevant dates in the sequence. When compared to those participants who did not receive training in countermeasures, Ganis et al. found that deception detection accuracy fell to only 33 percent in participants with countermeasures training. As a result, they conclude: "These findings show that fMRI-based deception detection methods can be vulnerable to countermeasures, calling for caution before applying these methods to real-world situations" (Ganis et al. 2011: 312).

A second critical issue discussed in the literature has to do with the fact that the vast majority of studies in this domain use artificial settings that guarantee experimental control at the expense of real-world validity (Greely and Illes 2007; Gamer 2014). As Gamer describes, "with the exception of very few studies . . ., participants were always instructed to lie to specific questions and were not free to decide about their behavior during the interrogation procedure" (2014: 178). Moreover, "participants had nothing to lose when failing the test which sharply contrasts with the situation in the field where test results might have devastating consequences for the examinee." It remains an open question, then, how neuroimaging techniques will fare in real-world situations where the stakes are high and laboratory controls are not possible.

A third concern has to do with the lack of diversity of subjects in these studies (Greely and Illes 2007; Rusconi and Mitchener-Nissen 2013). For the most part, these experiments used healthy young adults with little gender or ethnic diversity. "No one tested children, the middle-aged or elderly, those with physical or mental illnesses, or those taking drugs, either as medication or illicitly" (Greely and Illes 2007: 403). This is problematic since the criminal justice system interacts with many types of individuals that are not taken into account in these fMRI studies. For neuroimaging lie detection to be reliable in the real world, it needs to be "able to cope with the types of individuals usually encountered by law enforcement officers, including substance addicts, those with high incentives to lie, and those with mental disorders" (Rusconi and Mitchener-Nissen 2013: 6). The lack of extensive research on such populations is a huge drawback. In fact, doubts already exist as to whether fMRI would be usable for those presenting with conditions such as delusions and amnestic disorders with confabulation (Langleben et al. 2006).

A fourth concern has to do with the inconsistency of reported brain regions of activity in these studies. As Greely and Illes write: "[A]ll of the relevant experiments report finding activation of various regions of the brain (sometimes defined narrowly, sometimes broadly). Together, they find activation in many different areas of the brain without strong consistency among the experiments, except when brain regions are very broadly defined" (2007: 403). This diversity "casts some doubt on the accuracy of any particular method of lie detection" (Greely and Illes 2007: 403). The problem is that researchers cannot agree on *exactly which* brain regions denote deception, at least not with any degree of precision.

A closely related concern is that, given the diversity of brain regions identified in these studies, how are we to demonstrate which, if any, constitute the neural correlates of lying? Perhaps some of these regions are involved in subjects exerting extra effort, rather than being the neural correlate of the lie itself. After all, lying often requires extra effort compared to responding truthfully. Such extra effort may be aimed at inhibiting the truth and/or producing an alternative response that sounds realistic. Given the very real possibility, then, that some of these regions may be associated with tasks related to or involved in lying, but not lying itself, it would be very difficult to prove that a person is lying whenever a particular region activates during a task. In fact, "many defendants [while testifying] do inhibit their natural tendency to blurt out everything they know … Many of them also suppress expression of anger and outrage at accusations. Suppressing natural tendencies is not a reliable indicator of lying, in the context of trial" (Grafton et al. 2006: 36–37). Given that fMRIs merely detect and measure manifestations of thoughts through changes in oxygenated blood, which proponents consider denotes lying, "any exhibited increase in blood flow detected by fMRI may result from alternative neurological processes such as anxiety, fear, or other heightened emotional states which are unrelated to the question of deception" (Rusconi and Mitchener-Nissen 2013: 5). In other words, just because certain brain regions are activated during deception, it does not follow that every time those regions are activated the individual is lying.

Beyond these rather technical concerns, there are also important legal and ethical concerns that need to be considered. As Rusconi and Mitchener-Nissen write:

> The perverse irony for the cognitive neuroscientists who have been developing these new technologies in a conscious effort to address the legal shortcomings of polygraphs is that, while techniques like fMRI might well tick the boxes of reliability and objectivity when perfected, the solution of bypassing physiological responses in favor of the direct recording of neural activity may itself constitute grounds for the judiciary to reject neuroimaging technologies. Not because such solutions will necessarily lack reliability or objectivity, but because they potentially infringe on other human/constitutional rights and legal principles. The developers of neuroimaging technologies need to acknowledge and engage with these legal issues *before* they seek to impose their new techniques into criminal courts if they are to maximize their chances of winning over the already skeptical judicial gatekeepers. (2013: 7)

Among the legal and ethical concerns raised by neuroimaging technologies are possible constitutional and human rights violations regarding illegal search, right to silence, freedom of thought, right to privacy, human dignity, right to integrity of the person, and protection of personal data (see Rusconi and Mitchener-Nissen 2013; Greely and Illes 2007; Farahany 2023).

While I cannot discuss all these issues here, consider the question of whether fMRI-based lie detection constitutes a *search* of the subject, and if so, under what conditions such a search will be considered lawful or unlawful. Discussions in this area tend to center on the US Constitutional Fourth Amendment, which protects against unreasonable or unlawful searches. According to some commentators, neuroimaging techniques will constitute a legitimate search under established legal doctrine should neural activity be equated to other forms of physical evidence gathered from the human body, such as blood or DNA sampling, fingerprints, voice samples, etc. – provided that probable cause exists justifying such sampling. However, as Rusconi and Mitchener-Nissen note: "it is easy to conceptualize neural activity as distinct from other forms of physiological evidence" (2013: 8). For example, "while we can manipulate neural activity by conducting mathematical problems in our head, we cannot change our DNA profile through thought processes" (2013: 8). What legal weight such a distinction should carry has yet to be determined, but neurolaw practitioners need to be addressing these issues now.

Another question that needs to be considered is whether or not authorities should be allowed to record our neural activity without our consent. If it is determined, for instance, that neuroimaging-based lie detection is a search subject to Fourth Amendment regulation, government authorities can perform it as long as they obtain a warrant. But should the state be allowed to access private mental activity without consent? On the one hand, the courts may rule that neural activity is unlike other kinds of evidence and that neural-searches are a violation of individuals' privacy. On the other hand, the US Supreme Court has already ruled that in matters of public safety, some violations of privacy may be justified (*Katz* v. *United States* 389 US 347 [1967]). For instance, a defendant may sometimes be required to undergo diagnostic tests and even medical surgeries in order to seize potentially probative evidence such as a bullet or ingested jewelry (Aharoni et al. 2022). When confronted with this problem, courts will be forced to either shoehorn this new technology into existing legal frameworks governing conceptually similar subject matter (i.e., DNA, blood, fingerprints, etc.) or produce new bespoke legal frameworks for this governance (Rusconi and Mitchener-Nissen 2013: 8).

Another potential legal concern is whether fMRI questioning undermines the right to silence and the right not to self-incriminate. Rusconi and Mitchener-Nissen sketch the problem as follows:

> Neuroimaging technology has the potential to undermine these rights if it can operate without the individual needing to speak. Within the United States, the Supreme Court has previously speculated that "the involuntary transmission of incriminating lie-detection evidence would violate a suspect's right to silence" (Simpson 2008: 767). Under the European Convention on Human Rights (ECHR) whilst there is no explicit protection against self-incrimination, in the case of *Funke v France* (A/256-A; 1993; 1 C.M.L.R. 897, ECHR) the European Court of Human Rights (ECtHR) was explicit that the right not to self-incriminate is an implicit component of one's *Right to a fair trial* under Article 6 ECHR (Jackson 2009). The ECtHR in *Saunders v United Kingdom* (1997, 23 EHRR 313) drew a distinction between material which respects the will of the suspect to remain silent and materials which exist independent of the suspect's will such as DNA, blood, urine, and breath. Unfortunately, what they left for a future court to decide is whether or not an individual's brain activity exists independent of their will to remain silent? (2013: 9)

It's easy to see, then, that important moral and legal questions remain unanswered – not only with regard to the right to silence and what constitutes lawful search, but also with regard to other rights as well.

Because of concerns like these, some commentators have argued that what is needed is the recognition of a new set of "neurorights" (see McCay 2022; Farahany 2023). Advocates of neurorights maintain that we "must establish the right to cognitive liberty – to protect freedom of thought and rumination, mental privacy, and self-determination over our brains and mental experiences" (Farahany 2023: 11). But while the case for neurorights is sometimes made in light of neuroimaging-based lie detection, it is more often directed toward the use of neurotechnologies more generally (McCay 2022; Farahany 2023). *Neurotechnologies* are devices that monitor the brain or nervous systems of people, and may act on them to influence neural activity (McCay 2022). Sometimes neurotechnologies are implanted in the brain, or interact with the nervous system through a headset or another "wearable" device. They are used in research and in therapeutic contexts, in computer gaming, meditation, and sometimes in the workplace to monitor attention. The concern is that large amounts of "brain data" collected by neurotech devices could allow people, governments, and corporations with access to hack our brains, make inferences about our mental states, and potentially profit off of us. This raises concerns about mental privacy and commercial manipulation. It's important, therefore, that before we permit the use of neuroimaging-based lie detection in criminal courts, we first consider whether new neurorights protections are needed or whether existing rights and protections can sufficiently address the concerns just raised.

To summarize, while initial studies suggest that neuroimaging-based lie detection may one day become a viable alternative to current methods, we have a long way to go before its reliability and accuracy are proven effective enough for use in the real-world. Current fMRI-based studies on deception detection have shown promising results, but they are still vulnerable to countermeasures, use highly artificial settings, and lack the kind of diversity of subjects likely to be encountered within the criminal justice system. It's also unclear whether the kinds of lies tested in these studies resemble the full diversity of situations, settings, and kinds of lies found in the real world. Concerns also remain about the inconsistency of reported brain regions identified in these studies, as well as the difficulty of determining which regions constitute the neural correlates of lying – and not, say, regions associated with tasks related to, or involved in, lying. Beyond these concerns, there are also important ethical and legal issues that still need to be addressed. If neuroimaging methods were one day perfected, it does not automatically follow that we should permit their use in court. Accuracy and reliability are not the only issues. We also need to determine whether their use violates important human and constitutional rights.

3 Interventions

The second domain of neurolaw concerns various types of brain-based *interventions*, or what we can call "neurointerventions." Neurointerventions refer to a range of techniques or interventions that directly target the brain or nervous system to affect neurological functioning. These interventions can include medical procedures, treatments, or interventions that aim to alter brain activity, structure, or function for various purposes, such as medical treatment, crime prevention, rehabilitation, or enhancement. Some examples of neurointerventions include Deep Brain Stimulation (DBS) (a procedure where electrodes are implanted in specific brain regions and connected to a device that delivers electrical impulses to alleviate symptoms or neurological disorders like Parkinson's disease, essential tremor, and obsessive-compulsive disorder), neuropharmacology (the use of drugs or medications that directly affect the brain and nervous system to treat neurological conditions, mental illnesses, or cognitive enhancement), and Transcranial Magnetic Stimulation (TMS) (a noninvasive technique that uses magnetic fields to stimulate specific regions of the brain, commonly used to treat depression and investigate brain functions).

With regard to neurolaw, the kinds of neurointerventions most discussed include those aimed at reducing reoffending, rehabilitating criminals, or preventing crime before it occurs. In fact, various jurisdictions are already using techniques that would be classified as neurointerventions, and research suggests that potentially, an even wider range of rehabilitative neurointerventions may be developed (Shaw 2022: 1411). This section examines the ethical, legal, and philosophical concerns associated with neurointerventions, including worries over consent, privacy, rights, personal identity, equitable access, and potential misuse.

3.1 The Benefits of Neurointerventions

To begin, we should note that there are several potential benefits associated with the use of neurointerventions. First and foremost, neurointerventions have the potential to reduce crime, suffering, and financial and personal costs. Imprisonment comes at a high economic cost to society. The Bureau of Justice Statistics estimates that the United States alone spends more than $80 billion each year to keep roughly 2.3 million people behind bars – and many experts say that figure is a gross underestimate. Incarceration also comes at great personal cost to prisoners – including separation from family and friends, loss of liberty, and stigmatization. Hence, "if neurointerventions are developed to effectively aid criminal rehabilitation, then these interventions have the potential to generate economic savings and to spare offenders suffering by allowing them to avoid incarceration or be released earlier" (Shaw 2022: 1421; see also Shaw 2018a).

Neurointerventions also have the potential to assist in the treatment and rehabilitation of individuals involved in the criminal justice system. By addressing underlying neurological issues or enhancing cognitive functioning, these interventions potentially contribute to reducing the likelihood of recidivism. The potential of neurointerventions also extends beyond rehabilitation to the prevention of crime. By identifying individuals at risk through neurobiological markers, early intervention with targeted neurointerventions can disrupt the trajectory towards criminal behavior. This proactive approach, based on the underlying neurological factors, may contribute to crime prevention.

One of the most widely discussed and debated neurointerventions is "chemical castration," which is a medical intervention that involves the use of anti-libidinal medications to suppress or reduce sexual drive and functioning (Douglas et al. 2013; Douglas 2014a; Forsberg and Douglas 2017; Sifferd 2020; Shaw 2022). It is primarily used as a treatment for individuals who have committed sexual offenses, particularly those involving pedophilia or other forms of sexual violence. The term "castration" is used metaphorically here since the medications used do not physically remove or alter the genital organs – and unlike physical castration, chemical castration is generally reversible when treatment is discontinued (although it can produce permanent side effects). The medications used in chemical castration typically fall into two categories: anti-androgens and gonadotropin-releasing hormone (GnRH) agonists. Anti-androgens work by blocking the effects of androgens, such as testosterone, in the body. GnRH agonists, on the other hand, inhibit the release of gonadotropins, which are hormones that stimulate the production of testosterone or estrogen.

In the literature on neurointerventions, "anti-libidinal drugs that reduce the effects or production of testosterone are considered neurointerventions because they have a considerable impact on the brain and on aspects of the individual's psychology such as thoughts, desires, and motivations" (Shaw 2022: 1414). This is important since the effects of anti-libidinal drugs on the brain are more important in addressing sexual offending than the drugs' physical effects on sexual function (Greely and Farahany 2019). As Shaw correctly notes, "Even if someone's ability to engage in penetrative sexual activity has been reduced/removed, the person can still find ways of committing serious sexual offenses if the desire/motivation to do so remains" (2022: 1414–15). In theory, then, anti-libidinal drugs function as a neurointervention by moderating the activity of testosterone, which has effects on the responsiveness of both general and specific neurological arousal mechanisms, influences the processing of sexual sensory stimuli, and impacts the motivation, attention, and mood associated with aggression and dominance (Grubin 2018: 711–12).

Currently, a variety of jurisdictions administer anti-libidinal drugs to sex offenders "under either statutory provisions that specifically concern sexual behavior or general mental health legislation" (Shaw 2022: 1415). Depending on the jurisdiction, "these interventions may be offered on a voluntary basis within prison or in the community, imposed as a compulsory treatment in the community or as a mandatory condition of parole, or exchanged for early release" (Shaw 2022: 1415). For instance, several European countries allow for only the voluntary use of chemical castration, which means that it cannot be imposed as a compulsory penalty but can be offered as a treatment option or an alternative to further incarceration. In Poland, however, it is possible to sentence offenders to compulsory chemical castration. In 1996, California law was amended to require chemical castration for repeat child molesters upon parole (California Penal Code, Sect. 645).

While the use of chemical castration is controversial for a number of reasons, including concerns over consent, coercion, effectiveness, and side effects, I mention it here only to highlight one widely discussed neurointervention. In what follows, I'll discuss all the various concerns that arise with this and other forms of neurointervention, especially when they are mandated by the state rather than offered voluntarily. It's important to recognize, however, that neurointerventions are already being utilized within the criminal justice system to rehabilitate offenders and reduce recidivism. And while some neurointerventions are rather invasive and/or come with significant risks or side effects, others are rather benign and have very few, if any, side effects (Choy, Focquaert, and Raine 2020).

For instance, one rather benign form of intervention is the use of neurofeedback therapy in correctional settings. Neurofeedback is "an innovative approach that may ultimately lessen criminal behavior, prevent violence, and lower recidivism" (Gkotsi and Benaroyo 2012: 3). As Gkotsi and Benaroyo describe:

> Neurofeedback or neurotherapy is a relatively new, noninvasive method which is based on the possibility of training and adjusting the speed of brainwaves, which normally occur at various frequencies … An overabundance, or deficiency in one of these frequencies, often correlates with conditions such as depression, and emotional disturbances and learning disabilities, such as Attention Deficit Hyperactivity Disorder (ADHD) … Therapists attach electrodes to the patients' head and a device records electrical impulses in the brain. These impulses are sorted into different types of brain waves. Using a program similar to a computer game, patients learn to control the video display by achieving the mental state that produces increases in the desired brain wave activity. Neurofeedback has gained recognition for its potential benefits for children with ADHD, alcoholics and drug addicts. (2012: 3)

Douglas Quirk (1995), a Canadian researcher, tested the effects of a neurofeedback treatment program on seventy-seven dangerous offenders in an Ontario correctional institute who suffered from deep-brain epileptic activity. The results demonstrated a reduction in the subjects' criminal recidivism and suggested that "a subgroup of dangerous offenders can be identified, understood, and successfully treated using this kind of biofeedback conditioning program" (1995). Additional studies on juvenile offenders with significant psychopathology and electroencephalographic abnormalities (Smith and Sams 2005), and on male adolescents diagnosed with ADHD (Martin and Johnson 2005), also demonstrated reduced recidivism, improved cognitive performance, improved emotional and behavioral reactions, and inhibition of inappropriate responses. These results are promising and suggest that neurofeedback could potentially provide a noninvasive, cost-effective method for reducing recidivism.

Additional noninvasive forms of neurointerventions include transcranial magnetic stimulation, omega-3 supplementation, and mindfulness and meditation techniques. Something as benign as omega-3 supplements, for instance, has been proposed as a way to reduce aggression and antisocial behavior in children and adults (Raine et al. 2015; Choy, Focquaert, and Raine 2020) and studies have been conducted on its ability to reduce aggressive behavior in prison populations (Meyer et al. 2015; 202). Transcranial Magnetic Stimulation (TMS) and Transcranial Direct Current Stimulation (tDCS) are two additional promising noninvasive neurointerventions. TMS is a noninvasive form of brain stimulation that involves the use of magnetic fields to stimulate or inhibit specific brain regions through electromagnetic induction. During a TMS session, an electromagnetic coil is placed against the scalp, which creates a varying magnetic field, inducing a current within a region in the brain itself. It can be employed to target areas associated with impulse control, aggression, or emotional regulation, with the aim of reducing criminal behavior. tDCS, on the other hand, is used to modulate cortical excitability, producing facilitatory or inhibitory effects upon a variety of behaviors. The main differences between the two are that TMS uses repetitive electromagnetic pulses while tDCS uses a constant weak electrical current, TMS is a neuro-stimulator while tDCS is a neuro-modulator, and tDCS equipment is typically small, battery-powered, and portable, while TMS devices are wall-powered, larger, and heavier.

While the effectiveness of these neurointerventions in reducing criminal behavior is still an area of ongoing research, several studies have shown good results in addressing various behaviors associated with criminal conduct, such as aggression, anger, irritability, and impulsivity (see Romero-Martinez, Bressanutti, and Moya-Albiol 2020; Philipp-Wiegmann et al. 2011; Choy, Raine, and Hamilton 2018). For instance, in one study using transcranial direct current stimulation, stimulation of the dorsal anterior cingulate cortex resulted in improved performance on cognitive and affective attentional tasks (To et al. 2018). In another study using the same technology, a single stimulation session of the dorsolateral prefrontal cortex reduced the desire to carry out violent antisocial acts by over 50 percent (Choy, Raine, and Hamilton 2018). Studies by Fecteau et al. (2007) and Boggio et al. (2010) also found that stimulation of the left dorsolateral prefrontal cortex produced a decrease in risk-taking, a behavior associated with increased inhibitory control.

We can see, then, that neurointerventions have the potential to contribute to crime prevention in several ways. Some potential benefits include rehabilitation and recidivism reduction. By combining neurointerventions with therapy, counseling, or behavioral interventions, it may be possible to enhance treatment outcomes and reduce the likelihood of recidivism. Neurointerventions can also target and address underlying neurological issues that contribute to criminal behavior. By modulating brain activity or addressing imbalances, these interventions may help reduce impulsivity, aggression, or other behaviors linked to criminal conduct. Certain neurointerventions, such as cognitive training or neurofeedback, can also improve cognitive functioning and enhance self-regulation skills. These improvements can support individuals in making better decisions, managing emotions, and developing the necessary skills to avoid engaging in criminal activities. Finally, neurointerventions have the potential to provide personalized treatment plans based on an individual's neurobiological profile. This tailored approach can address specific cognitive or behavioral deficits that may contribute to criminal behavior, leading to more effective interventions.

3.2 Safety and Effectiveness

While the use of neurointerventions offers a number of promising benefits, it's important to note that addressing and reducing crime involves a complex interplay of various factors, including social, environmental, psychological, and economic aspects. Hence, the reduction of crime requires comprehensive approaches that involve social interventions, community support, evidence-based rehabilitative programs, and addressing underlying causes such as poverty, substance abuse, homelessness, and mental health issues (Caruso 2021a). While neurointerventions may have a role to play as part of a broader approach to crime, they alone do not constitute a comprehensive solution to crime reduction. Furthermore, the use of neurointerventions should be approached with caution since there are important ethical considerations that must first be addressed, including concerns over safety, consent and coercion, individual rights, and personal identity.

Henry Greely (2007), for instance, has argued that the use of neurointerventions within the criminal justice system is only acceptable if the interventions are safe and effective. Though this seems simple enough, we need to keep in mind that "when it comes to interventions against criminal behavior, proving safety and efficacy is fraught with difficulties" (2007: 1116). As Choy, Focquaert, and Raine note, "for many interventions, establishing adequate safety and effectiveness is challenging given that clinical trials in offender populations face serious hurdles due to practical, ethical, and regulatory limitations" (2020: 5). For instance, in many cases, psychopharmacological interventions "are known to be used off-label [not officially approved] in offender populations without guarantees concerning effectiveness in reducing recidivism or adequate implementation limitation to prevent irreversible side effects" (Choy, Focquaert, and Raine 2020: 33). To make things even more complicated, a significant number of offenders suffer from mental disorders and therefore face "double vulnerability."

If neurointerventions are to be used ethically, adequate safeguards are essential. One proposal, which I find reasonable, demands, minimally, that the treatment or neurointervention in question "must be considered standard medical therapy before its use is considered within the criminal justice system" (Choy, Focquaert, and Raine 2020: 33). This, at least, prohibits the use of experimental neurointerventions on offenders within the criminal justice system or off-label use of psychopharmacological interventions. I favor this approach over the more extreme option, which is to prohibit the use of all neurointerventions. That's because, if benign and effective biological interventions exist, not allowing offenders to benefit from these treatments would make an already vulnerable group even more vulnerable by excluding the possibility of a future crime-free life. Furthermore, as Neil Levy's *parity principle* stipulates: "Unless we can identify *ethically relevant* differences between internal and external interventions and alterations, we ought to treat them on a par" (2007: 62).

Of course, important questions still remain, such as *how* safe and effective must an intervention be proven before we consider it ethically acceptable? While I do not propose to answer this question here, I maintain that the same ethical considerations that guide the use of medical, biological, and psychopharmacological interventions in general should guide the use of neurointerventions within the criminal justice system more specifically. These include the medical ethical *principles of beneficence* and *nonmaleficence*. The principle of beneficence requires a moral obligation to act for the benefit of others. The principle of nonmaleficence, on the other hand, holds that there is an obligation not to inflict harm on others and is closely associated with the maxim *primum non nocere* (first do no harm). Since many treatments involve some degree of harm (e.g., side effects from drugs, chemotherapy, etc.), these principles are typically interpreted as implying that the harm should not be disproportionate to the reasonably expected benefits of treatment. While there are examples of neurointerventions that clearly run afoul of these principles and therefore should be prohibited, there will also be safe and effective neurointerventions that satisfy these principles.

For instance, pharmacological interventions for drug or alcohol addiction, in conjunction with other anti-addiction counseling and treatments, often produce, on the whole, a balance of benefits over risks/harms and can be quite effective in combating addiction. When this is the case, and these treatment programs use FDA-approved drugs to combat drug and alcohol addiction, we can say that they satisfy the principles of beneficence and nonmaleficence and are prima facie ethically permissible. Addiction to heroin or other opioids, for instance, can be treated with methadone, which prevents withdrawal symptoms and reduces the craving for heroin, while avoiding many of the risks and harms of heroin. In fact, abundant evidence shows that methadone, buprenorphine, and naltrexone all reduce opioid use and opioid use disorder-related symptoms, and that they reduce the risk of infectious disease transmission as well as criminal behavior associated with drug use (American Society for Addiction Medicine 2017; National Institute of Drug Abuse 2021). These medications also increase the likelihood that a person will remain in treatment, which itself is associated with a lower risk of overdose mortality, reduced risk of HIV and HCV transmission, reduced criminal justice involvement, and a greater likelihood of employment. While these drugs are not without side effects and risks, it is often thought that their benefits outweigh the risks. When this is the case, and these drugs are considered standard medical therapy and approved by the FDA, we may object to their use within the criminal justice system on other ethical grounds (e.g., consent and coercion), but not on the grounds of safety and effectiveness. It's the job of experts, therefore, to determine which types of interventions are safe and effective, when the benefits outweigh the costs, and when these interventions can be employed within the criminal justice system without exploiting vulnerable populations or violating other important ethical considerations.

3.3 Consent and Coercion

In addition to concerns over safety and effectiveness, the use of neurointerventions also raises complex questions about consent and coercion – especially among imprisoned populations. Consider, for instance, the *principle of autonomy*, another common medical ethical principle. In medical practice, autonomy is usually expressed as the right of competent adults to make informed decisions about their own medical care. The principle underlies the requirement of informed consent of patients before any investigation or treatment takes place. Two conditions are ordinarily required before a decision can be regarded as autonomous. The individual has to have the relevant internal capacities for self-government and has to be free from external constraints. Does the use of neurointerventions within the criminal justice system run afoul of the principle of autonomy? And, if so, is this ever justified?

To begin, I would first like to note that some theorists have argued that offering neurointerventions under the right circumstances can actually *increase* the autonomy and well-being of offenders (Douglas et al. 2013; Focquaert 2014; Ryberg 2019; Choy, Focquaert, and Raine 2020). As Choy and colleagues explain:

> Desires, cravings, and habits that motivate criminal behavior can be experienced as impediments to making autonomous choices. Biological treatments [and neurointerventions] that reduce the internal coercion that such desires and cravings produce have the potential to increase an individual's autonomy and ability to lead a crime-free life. (2020: 34)

Douglas et al., for instance, have argued that chemical castration can "increase future autonomy overall, either by removing internal barriers (such as irrational, inauthentic, compulsive desires) or external ones (such as restrictions on free movement)" (2013: 399). The thought here is that desires that drive many sex offenders frequently constitute very severe impediments to autonomy and are often at odds with the individual's own higher-order desires (not to offend, to remain ethical, and to resist their compulsive sexual desires). By removing (or reducing) these impediments, the individual's autonomy and authentic-self can be restored.

Derk Pereboom and I have made a similar point with regard to reasons-responsiveness (Pereboom and Caruso 2018). We maintain that methods of therapy that engage reasons-responsive abilities should always be preferred – for example, consoling, talk therapies, and educational programs. Still, a concern for many forms of therapy proposed for altering criminal tendencies is that they circumvent, rather than address, the criminal's capacity to respond to reasons. On our view:

> ... the fact that a mode of therapy circumvents rather than addresses the capacities that confer dignity on us should not all by itself make it illegitimate for agents who are in general responsive to reasons but not in particular respects. Imagine such an agent who is beset by bouts of violent anger that he cannot control in some pertinent sense. Certain studies suggest that this tendency is due to deficiencies in serotonin and that it can sometimes be alleviated by antidepressants. It would seem mistaken to claim that such a mode of treatment is illegitimate because it circumvents capacities for

rational and autonomous response. In fact, this sort of treatment often produced responsiveness to reasons where it was previously absent (Pereboom
2001). A person beset by violent anger will typically not be responsive to
certain kinds of reasons to which he would be responsive if he were not
suffering from this problem. Therapy of this sort can thus increase reasons-
responsiveness. (2018: 211)

By analogy, we argue that one standard form of treatment for alcoholism –
which many alcoholics voluntarily undergo – involves the use of Antabuse,
which makes one violently ill after the ingestion of alcohol. By counteracting
addictive alcoholism, this drug can result in enhanced autonomy and reasons-
responsiveness.

According to Pereboom and me, treatments and interventions that increase
reasons-responsiveness in this way are ethical if carried out in a way that respects
autonomy by leaving the decision up to the offender. Some ethicists worry,
however, that if an offender is presented with a choice between accepting
a particular intervention/drug/treatment or facing the prospect of further incarceration if they refuse, their consent is not valid since it is partly coerced. While this is
a difficult issue that deserves more attention than I can give it here, my short reply
would be that, although incarcerated offenders clearly face pressure to consent in
such situations, that pressure does not render their consent invalid because their
choice is still sufficiently voluntary (Bomann-Larsen 2011; Wertheimer and Miller
2014; Ryberg 2019). In fact, there is some evidence that the conditions under
which crime-preventing interventions are agreed to by incarcerated offenders are
not perceived as coercive by the offenders themselves (Poythress et al. 2002; Rigg
2002; Moser et al. 2004; Redlich et al. 2010; Douglas et al. 2013: n4).

But what about those interventions that are mandated by the court or made
a requirement for release? Even here, some ethicists have argued that mandated
neurointerventions and mandated incarceration can be comparable responses to
crime, thereby holding that liability to incarceration implies liability to some
forms of forced interventions (Douglas 2014a; Ryberg 2019). Thomas Douglas
(2014a), for instance, questions the need to obtain informed consent for using
neurointerventions (or what he calls "medical correctives") on offenders. He
writes: "Why is it that, following offending, consent is required for the impos-
ition of medical correctives, but not for these more traditional kinds of criminal
remedy [incarceration, psychological rehabilitation programs, fines, community service, probation regimes, and the freezing of financial assets]?" (2014a:
105). According to Douglas:

> . . . if locking offenders in prison for a long period of time is justified, then it's
> difficult to see why requiring prisoners to undergo some type of safe and
> effective neurointervention couldn't also be acceptable. In many cases

neurointerventions may be less intrusive and harmful, and potentially more effective in preventing reoffending, which is normally at least one of the purported purposes of incarceration. (2014b)

Douglas's argument, therefore, maintains that if the goals of rehabilitation, crime prevention, and security can justify mandatory minimal incarceration, they can also justify some nonconsensual neurointerventions.

Given that most academics debating the ethics of neurointerventions share the assumption that administering interventions to offenders without their valid consent would be unethical – disagreeing only over whether offenders can, in fact, *validly* consent in certain coercive circumstances – Douglas's challenge to the "consent requirement" (2014a: 104) is a significant one. If it succeeds, it would have major implications for the nonconsensual use of neurointerventions. There are, however, a number of powerful objections to this view (see Shaw 2018b, 2019; Choy, Focquaert, and Raine 2020).

First, forced neurointerventions violate an individual's right to bodily integrity, and the forced nature of the intervention, in and of itself, can be experienced as invasive, degrading, and humiliating (Shaw 2019; Choy, Focquaert, and Raine 2020: 34). Elizabeth Shaw (2019), for instance, questions whether even the supposedly benign proposal of compulsory injections is unlikely to cause serious harm. She writes:

> Douglas claims it is doubtful that compulsory injections of prisoners would be experienced in seriously negative ways, since healthcare workers and children do not find their experience of compulsory (or strongly encouraged) vaccinations an extremely negative experience. However, there are reasons for thinking that prisoners might experience these injections differently from children and healthcare workers ... [For one,] [t]he offender is likely to doubt whether the injections will promote his own welfare. Furthermore, the thought of being forcibly injected with a chemical that alters one's motivations in a way that bypasses one's rational faculties could be particularly distressing. (Shaw 2019: 103)

To further complicate matters, given the wide discrepancy in human experiences, "it will be nearly impossible to outline general rules of practice based on the level of intrusiveness and harm that either incarceration or biological intervention entails" (Choy, Focquaert, and Raine 2020: 35).

Second, Shaw (2018b, 2019) argues that the mandatory injection of prisoners poses a *communicative* threat to agency – that is, "Pinning someone down and forcibly injecting her with a mind-altering drug is likely to send out a more disrespectful message about the individual than incarceration would" (2019: 104). She goes on to argue:

> Violating bodily (and mental) integrity sends out a disrespectful message, because it invades a particular intimate sphere. The individual's body and mind are *constitutive* of the person and invading the mind and body therefore amounts to a fundamental attack on the person, in a way that interfering with free movement does not. (2019: 104)

The problem is that suggesting that consent for neurointerventions is the default ethical requirement for all competent adults under normal circumstances, but not for offenders, "signals to offenders that they are somehow less deserving of respect as persons compared to nonoffenders" (Choy, Focquaert, and Raine 2020: 35). In my opinion, this is a powerful reason to object to nonconsensual interferences with both bodily and mental integrity.

For the foregoing reasons, I oppose the use of mandated or forced neurointerventions. The best way to respect the autonomy of competent adults, I contend, is to leave decisions about neurointerventions up to the individual. Mandated neurointerventions interfere with the rights of mental and bodily integrity – and violating mental and bodily integrity is generally more disrespectful and harder to justify than interfering with freedom of movement (Shaw 2018b, 2019). While I understand that concerns about consent still remain for incarcerated offenders, it's not clear that leaving the option up to the individual for safe and effective neurointerventions should be ruled out as morally illegitimate. This is because the offender's choice is, I contend, still sufficiently voluntary in most circumstances. This is especially true when the neurointerventions in question are noninvasive and rather benign, like neurofeedback therapy.

But what about those neurointerventions that are more invasive, like chemical castration? And what if the only legitimate alternative to continued incarceration is for the offender to choose chemical castration? For me, a lot will depend on how safe and effective chemical castration is ultimately proven – which remains an open empirical question (Rice and Harris 2003). Some small-scale, controlled studies have found that chemical castration, administered using cyproterone acetate (CPA) and medroxyprogesterone acetate (MPA), is effective in reducing recidivism in sexual offenders with paraphilias (Fedoroff et al. 1992; Maletzky, Tolan, and McFarlan 2006). However, other studies have found no significant effect (Hucker, Langevin, and Bain 1988). On the other hand, "several studies have shown high efficacy rates for GnRH agonists in dramatically reducing testosterone levels and self-reported deviant sexual desires and behaviors, including in individuals who did not respond to CPA or MPA" (Douglas et al. 2013: 395). But even here, more empirical studies are needed. Assuming for the moment, though, that chemical castration *was* proven sufficiently safe and effective, it's not clear that under such circumstances the moral problems with it are not outweighed if it is carried out in a way that respects autonomy by leaving the decision up to the individual.

3.4 Personal Identity

Another common concern about neurointerventions has to do with personal identity. Neurointerventions that alter brain function or modify cognitive processes may raise questions about the authenticity of a person's thoughts, emotions, or behaviors. If these interventions significantly change or manipulate core aspects of an individual's identity, it can lead to a sense of inauthenticity or perceived loss of self. Furthermore, altering brain function through neurointerventions can potentially disrupt the continuity of a person's identity. If the interventions cause a significant shift in personality, memories, or cognitive abilities, it may challenge the individual's sense of continuity over time, potentially leading to a feeling of disconnection from their past self. For these reasons, "One of the most salient worries related to personal identity is the fear of creating a *new person*, or radically changing a person's self up to the point where they can no longer consider themselves the same" (Focquaert and DeRidder 2009: 1). It's important, then, that we examine whether neurointerventions threaten our personal identity and if the possibility of identity changes provides a sound ethical argument against these techniques.

Before answering this question directly, it's important to note that a good deal of personal identity-related worries regarding neurointerventions rest upon a conflation of narrative and numerical identity. As Focquaert and DeRidder explain:

> Issues concerning personal identity through time or the *persistence question* are about numerical identity. The persistence question asks under what possible circumstances a person who exists at one time is identical to someone (or something) existing at another time? ... It therefore asks whether or not an individual is one and same *despite* change ... [On the other hand,] [i]ssues concerning narrative identity or the *characterization question* focus on the characteristics that truly or genuinely constitute a person's identity. (2009: 2)

Focquaert and DeRidder go on to claim that: "While it is self-evident that altering an individual's numerical identity is wrong, it is much less clear that altering one's narrative identity is ethically problematic" (2009: 2). This is because, while radical narrative changes are potentially problematic, mild identity changes are not necessarily problematic. In fact, "Mild and moderate narrative identity changes are part of our daily life and may result from a variety of life-changing experiences or circumstances."

For example, the "loss of a loved one may change someone from being optimistic to being depressed and without hope." Of course, narrative identity changes induced by neurointerventions come about differently, "but [they] are essentially the same as those that come about just by living our daily lives"

(Focquaert and DeRidder 2009: 2). Whether or not such changes are problematic depends on how much change in narrative identity (including changes in cognition, personality traits, emotions, and mood) is deemed "too radical" and a threat to personal identity.

Before investigating concerns about narrative identity further, let me just note that while it is self-evident that altering an individual's numerical identity is wrong, there is also a good reason to think that personal identity through time (numerical identity) is not threatened by neurointerventions in the same way as narrative identity. Numerical identity revolves around the necessary and sufficient conditions for a person at one point in time to be the same person at another point in time. And while philosophers do not fully agree on what these conditions are, two leading approaches focus on *psychological* and *biological continuity*:

> Psychological approaches describe these conditions in terms of continuity of psychological connections or experiential contents, such as memory or earlier experiences (i.e., episodic memory) or continuity of basic psychological capacities such as basic capacities for reasoning or consciousness. Biological approaches describe these conditions in terms of continuity of biological life. (Focquaert and DeRidder 2009: 2)

There is no reason to think, however, that neurointerventions threaten continuity in either of these senses (see Glannon 2007; Focquaert and DeRidder 2009) since neurointerventions do not affect the continuity of one's biological life and are "unlikely [to] affect the continuity of one's psychological connectedness or one's basic psychological capacities" (Focquaert and DeRidder 2009: 2). We can say, then, that "Philosophical and ethical worries about personal identity are typically about cases in which [neurointerventions are] successful in alleviating the patient's symptoms, but at the same time lead to changes in one's mental states (e.g., changes in personality traits)" (Focquaert and DeRidder 2009: 2). Such worries are therefore about changes in narrative identity rather than numerical identity (Glannon 2007).

What, then, can current findings on neurointerventions tell us about their effects on cognition, personality traits, emotions, and mood? That is, "which aspects of our narrative identity are (likely or unlikely) altered due to stimulation for neurological and neuropsychiatric disorders? Do these alterations involve drastic changes? And if yes, are such changes common?" (Focquaert and DeRidder 2009: 2). To help answer these questions, consider the use of DBS to treat Parkinson's disease. We can use this as a test case to see what personality changes, if any, are produced by DBS. Focquaert and DeRidder nicely summarize the key empirical findings as follows:

[W]ith respect to personality traits, Castelli et al. (2006) found a small improvement in obsessive compulsive and paranoid personality traits (7% experienced a postoperative worsening, while 20% showed a clinically relevant improvement). Other personality traits (e.g., antisocial, schizoid) remained stable . . . . Although disturbances (e.g., worsening of anxiety and mood) in individual cases are found, overall, patients experienced small improvements in mood and specific personality traits. Extreme disturbances (e.g., psychosis) are relatively rare. Houeto et al. (2006) report no changes in patient's personality traits or any adverse psychiatric effects following . . . DBS, based upon self-reported questionnaires, in 20 patients with [Parkinson's disease]. A more recent study by Castelli et al. (2008) (n=14) using an explorative test suggests "that there is no evidence of personality change in [Parkinson disease] patients submitted to STN-DBS" (p.8). Specially, regarding personality traits, mood and related changes, Witt et al. (2008) found that anxiety was significantly reduced, and mood slightly elevated in the DBS (n=60) . . . There were no significant changes after DBS in psychiatry scale scores, and an overall improvement in depression was found (although the effect size was small). (2009: 3)

None of these personality changes seem "radical" enough to constitute a significant threat to narrative personal identity. In fact, these findings show that "mild to moderate changes in one's narrative identity are observed in individual cases, while radical narrative changes are rare" (Focquaert and DeRidder 2009: 4). The same seems to be true for the use of DBS to treat neuropsychiatric disorders (see Focquaert and DeRidder 2009). It would therefore seem that changes in personality traits, emotions, and mood due to DBS are relatively uncommon in both Parkinson's disease and neuropsychiatric disorders.

Similar assessments would need to be done for other neurointerventions to determine whether or not they result in the kind of radical changes that threaten narrative personal identity. For most forms of noninvasive neurointerventions, like neurofeedback and transcranial magnetic stimulation, there's good reason to think that this will not be the case. Neurofeedback, for instance, does not radically change an individual's personality; it simply trains their brain to work more effectively and enhance their overall mental balance and mood. Dalkner et al. (2017), for example, studied the short-term beneficial effects of twelve sessions of neurofeedback on avoidant personality accentuation[3] in the treatment of alcohol use disorder and found that, while neurofeedback intervention had a positive effect on avoidant personality accentuation, there were no changes in other personality accentuations or in global Big Five personality dimensions after neurofeedback training. Raymond et al. (2005) similarly found

---

[3] Avoidant personality disorder is characterized by feelings of extreme social inhibition, inadequacy, and sensitivity to negative criticism and rejection.

that nine sessions of neurofeedback for participants with high scores for with-drawal led to improvements in mood (i.e., feeling more composed, agreeable, elevated, and confident) but were "insufficient to change personality" (2005: 287). Similarly, research on the relationship between personality traits and responses to Transcranial Magnetic Stimulation (TMS) treatments has found that although certain personality traits using the five-factor personality assess-ment were correlated with clinical remission (i.e., elimination) of depression symptoms, there were no changes in personality measures following a four-week course of TMS (McGirr et al. 2014).

None of this is to say, of course, that neurointerventions can never threaten personal identity, since there very may well be brain implants or neurosurgeries that do or can result in radical changes in narrative personal identity. It has been widely reported, for instance, that the historical use of lobotomies to treat psychiatric disorders, while not only dangerous, often resulted in radical changes in personality – that is, many people lost their ability to feel emotions and became apathetic, unengaged, and unable to concentrate (some even became catatonic) (see Caruso and Sheehan 2017). If we want to be certain that we are using neurointerventions in an ethical manner, we therefore need to be constantly assessing the empirical effects of neurointerventions on personal-ity traits, emotions, and mood, so as to avoid neurointerventions that bring about radical changes in narrative identity.

4 Revision

In this final section, I conclude by investigating the various ways neuroscience may impact the law by changing or *revising* commonsense views about human nature and the causes of human action. In particular, I focus on what the behavioral, cognitive, and neuroscience – and our modern scientific understanding of the mind/ brain, more generally – can tell us about free will, moral responsibility, and legal punishment. As we saw in the opening section, some theorists maintain that neuroscience shows that free will is an illusion, and therefore nobody is truly responsible for their actions. Therefore criminal law has to be revised (Greene and Cohen 2004; Alces 2018). Others maintain that neuroscience is completely irrelevant to criminal law and, hence, no major revisions are necessary (Morse 2005, 2013, 2018). In contrast with both these views, I will argue that, while neuroscience cannot itself disprove free will, it can provide important needlepoint to the *philosophical* arguments against free will. It can also help resolve some of the internal empirical constraints placed on different accounts of free will.

I begin with a short section on how neuroscience is already bringing about revision in the law. I then turn to a discussion of the relevance of free will to the criminal law and closely examine two distinct routes to *free will skepticism* – the position that doubts or denies that agents have the kind of control in action, that is, free will, needed for basic desert moral responsibility. The first route denies the causal efficacy of the types of willing required for free will and receives its contemporary impetus from pioneering work in neuroscience by Benjamin Libet, Daniel Wegner, and John Dylan Haynes. The second, which is more common in the philosophical literature, does not deny the causal efficacy of the will but instead claims that whether this causal efficacy is deterministic or indeterministic, it does not achieve the level of control to count as free will by the standards of the historical debate. I argue that while there are compelling objections to the first route (the neuroscientific route), the second route to free will skepticism remains intact. I then conclude by considering the different ways the criminal law might be revised in light of these arguments.

4.1 Neuroscience Is Already Revising the Law

To begin, it is important to recognize that developments in neuroscience have already begun to bring about changes and revisions in the law. One historical example can be found in the mid-twentieth century with the use of electroenceph-alography (EEG) to expand the rights of epileptics. As Francis Shen writes, "Epilepsy had 'plagued mankind from time immemorial,' and twenty-eight states had sterilization laws that included epileptics. As late as 1956, some states still had laws that restricted marriage of epileptics. But the 'discovery [of EEG] ... released epilepsy from the crypt of the unknown'" (2016: 676). Before EEG, and until the 1950s, individuals with epilepsy were legally denied the right to marry, the right to drive a car, and the right to obtain employment. Gradually, such laws targeting epileptics came under attack as lawyers and doctors banded together. These changes in the law "owed much to the discovery and application of EEG." Early on, EEGs were particularly useful in the diagnosis and treatment of epilepsy and related seizure disorders. And in 1956, a landmark book by Roscoe Barrow and Howard Fabing was published named *Epilepsy and Law: A Proposal for Legal Reform in the Light of Medical Progress*. Publications such as this contrib-uted to a series of legal reforms, "including giving epileptics the right to marry and drive cars with fewer restrictions." The reform of laws governing epilepsy clearly demonstrates that advances in neuroscience "can lead to positive legal and social outcomes" (Shen 2016: 679).

Another area where neuroscientific findings have, and are continuing to have, an effect on the law is in juvenile justice policy. Developmental psychologists Laurence Steinberg and Elizabeth Scott have argued, for instance, that juveniles are "less guilty by reason of adolescence" (2003: 1009). Under principles of criminal law, culpability is mitigated when the agent's decision-making capacity is diminished, when the criminal act was coerced, or when the act was out of character. Steinberg and Scott argue that juveniles should not be held to the same standards of criminal responsibility as adults because adolescents' decision-making capacity is diminished, they are less able to resist coercive influence, and their character is still undergoing change. The uniqueness of immaturity as a mitigating condition, they argue, suggests "commitment to a legal environment under which most youths are dealt with in a separate justice system and none are eligible for capital punishment."

The American Psychological Association (APA) agrees with this assessment and has partnered with jurisdictions nationwide to revise juvenile sentencing policies to align with developmental science (Abrams 2022). Their efforts have led to a series of amicus briefs, heavily cited in the US Supreme Court's *Roper* v. *Simmons* decision – which said using the death penalty before age eighteen was unconstitutional – and the subsequent *Graham* v. *Florida*, *Miller* v. *Alabama*, and *Jackson* v. *Hobbs* decisions, which collectively outlawed sentencing people under eighteen to life in prison without the possibility of parole. In the *Roper* case, the Court admitted MRI and other neuroscientific evidence showing the absence of frontal lobe maturation in the brains of teenagers (frontal lobes are causally implicated in decision-making and the control of impulse reactions). The Court cited three relevant ways that adolescents differ from adults: lack of maturity, increased impulsivity, and limited judgment; increased vulnerability and susceptibility to external pressure and negative influences; and a personality structure that is less fixed and more open to change. This led the US Supreme Court to rule that the Eighth and Fourteenth Amendments forbid the execution of offenders who were younger than age eighteen when the crime occurred.

The APA is now working to extend these legal reforms further. Drawing on an updated body of research on developmental psychology and neuroscience, a recent APA Presidential Task Force recommended the extension of these protections beyond age 18. In August 2022, the APA Council of Representatives approved the policy resolution with overwhelming support. "The fundamental argument is that the research the *Roper* court relied on to exclude seventeen-year-olds from eligibility for death as a penalty also applies at ages 18, 19, and 20," said Cecil Reynolds, the leader of the APA task force (as quoted in Abrams 2022: 49). In addition to the policy brief, the task force is creating an amicus brief for the Supreme Court and a tool kit for practitioners working with 18-, 19-, and 20-year-olds facing a death penalty charge. Psychologists and neuroscientists have also summarized research on brain development and trauma to inform other policy initiatives, including advocating for states to ban solitary confinement of juveniles and to raise the minimum age for trying children in the juvenile justice system.

4.2 Free Will and Its Relevance to the Law

In addition to laws governing epilepsy and juvenile justice, some theorists have proposed that advances in neuroscience will result in even more radical revisions to the law. These theorists argue that as our neuroscientific grasp of complex behavior improves, it will undermine our commonsense notions of free will and moral responsibility. Joshua Greene and Jonathan Cohen (2004) have argued, for instance, that the advance of neuroscience will eventually result in the widespread rejection of free will – and, with it, of retributivism. In their now classic paper, they argue:

> Cognitive neuroscience, by identifying the specific mechanisms responsible for behavior, will vividly illustrate what until now could only be appreciated through esoteric theorizing: that there is something fishy about our ordinary conceptions of human action and responsibility, and that, as a result, the legal principles we have devised to reflect these conceptions may be flawed. (2004: 1775)

According to Greene and Cohen, "The net effect of this influx of scientific information, will be the rejection of free will as it is ordinarily conceived, with important ramifications for the law" (2004: 1776). In particular, they argue that neuroscience will dramatically and beneficially change our legal system by forcing it to take cognizance of developments in our understanding of human capacities. This process will move it and us away from our retributive urges and toward a more compassionate consequentialist form of punishment in the future. They go on to propose that consequentialist reforms are in order, and they predict such reforms will take place.

But before examining the various neuroscientific and philosophical arguments against free will, it's important that we first acknowledge and fully appreciate the relevance of free will to the criminal law. First and foremost, the criminal law is founded on the idea that persons can be held morally responsible for their actions because they have freely chosen them. The US Supreme Court, for instance, has asserted:

> A "universal and persistent" foundation stone in our system of law, and particularly in our approach to punishment, sentencing, and incarceration, is the "belief in freedom of the human will and a consequent ability and duty of the normal individual to choose between good and evil." (*United States v. Grayson*, 438 U.S. 41 at 52 [1978], quoting *Morissette* v. *United States*, 342 U.S. 246, 250 [1952])

Indeed, the US courts have observed that "[t]he whole presupposition of the criminal law is that most people, most of the time, have free will within broad limits"[4] and that "the law has been guided by a robust common sense which assumes the freedom of the will as a working hypothesis in the solution of its problems."[5]

Free will is also relevant to criminal law because of the important role it plays, historically and currently, in one of the most prominent justifications of legal punishment: *retributivism*. The retributive justification of legal punishment maintains that, absent any excusing conditions, wrongdoers are morally responsible for their actions and *deserve* to be punished in proportion to their wrongdoing. Unlike theories of punishment that aim at deterrence, rehabilitation, or incapacitation, retributivism grounds punishment in the *blameworthiness* and *desert* of offenders. It holds that punishing wrongdoers is intrinsically good. For the retributivist, wrongdoers deserve a punitive response proportional to their wrongdoing, even if their punishment serves no further purpose. This backward-looking focus on *desert* is a central feature of most pure retributive accounts of punishment. And it is important to emphasize that the desert invoked in retributivism (in the classical or strict sense) is *basic* in the sense that it is not in turn grounded in forward-looking reasons such as securing the safety of society or the moral improvement of criminals. Thus, for the retributivist, the claim that persons are morally responsible for their actions in the *basic desert* sense is crucial to the state's justification for giving them their just deserts in the form of punishment for violations of the state's laws.

Given the importance, then, that assumptions about free will and basic desert moral responsibility play in the criminal law, if it turns out that agents lack free will, then major aspects of our criminal law and justice systems are unjustified. It's imperative, then, that we examine the neuroscientific and philosophical arguments against free will since one reason to think that no one ever deserves legal punishment, as retributivism presupposes, is that we lack the control in action, that is, the free will, required for moral responsibility in the basic desert sense.

4.3 Neuroscience and Free Will

In the literature, two prominent routes to free will skepticism are identifiable. The first, which is more prominent among scientific skeptics, maintains that recent findings in neuroscience reveal that unconscious brain activity causally initiates action prior to the conscious awareness of the intention to act, and that

---

[4] *Smith v. Amontrout*, 865 F.2d 1502, 1506 (8th Cir. 1988).
[5] *Steward Machine Co. v. Davis*, 301 U.S. 548. 590 (1937).

this indicates conscious will is an illusion. The pioneering work in this area was done by Benjamin Libet and his colleagues. In their groundbreaking study on the neuroscience of movement, Libet et al. (1983) investigated the timing of brain processes and compared them to the timing of conscious will in relation to self-initiated voluntary acts, and found that the conscious intention to move (which they labeled W) came 200 milliseconds before the motor act, but 350–400 milliseconds after the *readiness potential* (RP) – a ramplike buildup of electrical activity that occurs in the brain and precedes actual movement. Libet and others have interpreted this as showing that the conscious intention or decision to move cannot be the cause of action because it comes too late in the neuropsychological sequence (Libet 1985, 1999). According to Libet, since we become aware of an intention to act only after the onset of preparatory brain activity, the conscious intention cannot be the true cause of the action.

Libet's findings, in conjunction with additional findings by John Dylan Haynes (Soon et al. 2008) and others, have led some theorists to conclude that conscious will is an illusion and plays no important causal role in how we act (see Wegner 2002). Haynes and his colleagues, for example, were able to build on Libet's work by using functional magnetic resonance imaging (fMRI) to predict with 60 percent accuracy whether subjects would press a button with either their right or left hand up to ten seconds before the subject became aware of having made that choice (Soon et al. 2008). For some, the findings of Libet and Haynes are enough to threaten our conception of ourselves as free and responsible agents since they appear to undermine the causal efficacy of the types of willing required for free will.

There are, however, at least three reasons for thinking that these neuroscientific arguments for free will skepticism are unsuccessful.[6] First, there is no direct way to tell which conscious phenomena, if any, correspond to which neural events. In particular, in the Libet studies, it is difficult to determine what the RP corresponds to – for example, is it an intention formation or decision, or is it merely an urge of some sort? Al Mele (2009) has argued that the RP that precedes action by a half-second or more need not be construed as the cause of the action. Instead, it may simply mark the beginning of forming an *intention* to act. According to Mele, "it is much more likely that what emerges around – 500 ms is a *potential cause* of a proximal intention or decision than a proximal intention or decision itself" (2009: 51). On this interpretation, the RP is more accurately characterized as an "urge" to act or a preparation to act. I agree with Mele that this leaves open the possibility that conscious intentions can still be

---

[6] These objections first appeared in Pereboom and Caruso (2018). See also Björnsson and Pereboom (2014).

causes – that is, if the RP does not correspond to the formation of an intention or decision, but rather an urge, then it remains open that the intention formation or decision is a conscious event.

Second, almost everyone on the contemporary scene who believes we have free will, whether compatibilist or libertarian, also maintains that freely willed actions are caused by virtue of a chain of events that stretch backward in time indefinitely. At some point in time, these events will be such that the agent is not conscious of them. Thus, all free actions are caused, at some point in time, by unconscious events. However, as Eddy Nahmias (2011) correctly points out, the concern for free will raised by Libet's work is that *all* of the relevant causing of action is (typically) nonconscious, and consciousness is not causally efficacious in producing action. Given determinist compatibilism, however, it is not possible to establish this conclusion by showing that nonconscious events that precede conscious choice causally determine action since such compatibilists hold that every case of action will feature such events and that this is compatible with free will. And, given most incompatibilist libertarianisms, it is also impossible to establish this conclusion by showing that there are nonconscious events that render actions more probable than not by a factor of 10 percent chance (Soon et al. 2008) since almost all such libertarians hold that free will is compatible with such indeterminist causation by unconscious events at some point in the causal chain.

Furthermore, Neil Levy raises a related objection when he criticizes Libet's *impossible demand* (2005) that only consciously initiated actions could be free. Levy correctly argues that this presupposition places a condition upon freedom of action which is, in principle, impossible to fulfill for reasons that are entirely conceptual and have nothing to do, per se, with Libet's empirical findings. As Levy notes, "Exercising this kind of control would require that we control our control system, which would simply cause the same problem to arise at a higher-level or initiate an infinite regress of controllings" (2005: 67). If the unconscious initiation of actions is incompatible with control over them, then free will is impossible on conceptual grounds. Thus, Libet's experiments do not constitute a separate, empirical challenge to our freedom.

Finally, several critics have correctly noted the unusual nature of the Libet-style experimental situation – that is, one in which a conscious intention to flex at some time in the near future is already in place, and what is tested for is the specific implementation of this general decision. Nahmias (2011), for example, convincingly points out that it is often the case – when, for instance, we drive or play sports or cook meals – that we form a conscious intention to perform an action of a general sort, and subsequent specific implementations are not preceded by more specific conscious intentions. But, in such cases, the general conscious intention is very plausibly playing a key causal role. In Libet-style situations, when the instructions are given, subjects form conscious intentions to flex at some time or other, and, if it turns out that the specific implementations of these general intentions are not in fact preceded by specific conscious intentions, this would be just like the kinds of driving and cooking cases Nahmias cites. It seems that these objections cast serious doubts on the potential for neuroscientific studies to undermine the claim that we have the sort of free will at issue.

For the foregoing reasons, I reject this kind of neuroscientific argument against free will. Of course, doing so does not mean that there are not other, better arguments against free will. In fact, I will now present what I take to be the strongest and most compelling case for free will skepticism – one that does not appeal to epiphenomenalism or the timing of conscious processes.

4.4 Hard-Incompatibilism

In the past, the standard argument for free will skepticism was based on the notion of *determinism* – the thesis that facts about the remote past in conjunction with the laws of nature entail that there is only one unique future. *Hard determinists* argued that determinism is true and incompatible with free will and basic desert moral responsibility, either because it precludes the *ability to do otherwise* (leeway incompatibilism) or because it is inconsistent with one's being the "ultimate source" of action (source incompatibilism). For hard determinists, libertarian free will is an impossibility because human actions are part of a fully deterministic world and compatibilism is operating in bad faith. The hard determinist invokes the naturalistic consideration that everything that happens, including all of our actions, is made inevitable by the remote past physical events together with the laws of nature. It maintains that human beings are situated in a natural world of law-governed causes and effects, and as a result our character and actions are conditioned by causes that we do not control, including our genetic make-up, our upbringing, and the physical environment. Because of these general features of the universe, the hard determinist maintains that we cannot have the sort of control in action required for basic desert attributions.

While hard determinism had its classic statement in the time when Newtonian physics reigned, it has very few defenders today – largely because the development of quantum mechanics diminished confidence in determinism, for the reason that it has indeterministic interpretations. This is not to say that determinism has been refuted or falsified by modern physics, because it has not. In fact, a number of leading interpretations of quantum mechanics are consistent with determinism (see Bohm 1952; Vaidman 2014; Lewis 2016). It is also important to keep in mind that even if we allow some indeterminacy to exist at the microlevel of the universe, the level studied by quantum mechanics, there may still remain determinism-where-it-matters – that is, at the ordinary level of choices and actions, and even the electrochemical activity in our brains. Nevertheless, most contemporary free will skeptics now offer arguments that are agnostic about determinism (see Pereboom 2001, 2014; Levy 2011; Strawson 1986; Caruso 2012, 2021a).

My own variety of free will skepticism maintains that *whatever* the fundamental nature of reality – whether it be deterministic or indeterministic – we lack free will (Pereboom 2001, 2014; Caruso 2012, 2021a). This is because, while determinism is incompatible with free will, so too is any sort of indeterminism that has a good chance of being true. A more accurate name for this position would therefore be *hard incompatibilism* (Pereboom 2001, 2014), to differentiate it from hard determinism. Hard incompatibilism amounts to a rejection of both compatibilism and libertarianism. It maintains that the sort of free will required for basic desert moral responsibility is incompatible with causal determination by factors beyond the agent's control and also with the kind of indeterminacy in action required by the most plausible versions of libertarianism.

I contend that the most direct and convincing route to this conclusion runs as follows. Against the view that free will is compatible with the causal determination of our actions by natural factors beyond our control, I argue that there is no relevant difference between this prospect and our actions being causally determined by manipulators. Against libertarian views that appeal only to indeterminate events and states of the agent to preserve free will, I advance the *disappearing agent objection*, according to which agents are left unable to settle whether a decision occurs and hence cannot have the control required for basic desert moral responsibility. In response, some libertarians appeal to a more robust notion of causation according to which free will requires an agent, qua substance, to be irreducibly causally involved. While such accounts could, in theory, supply the control needed for basic desert moral responsibility, I argue that they cannot be reconciled with our best philosophical and scientific accounts of the world and face additional problems accounting for mental causation. Since this exhausts the options for views on which we have the sort of free will at issue, I conclude that free will skepticism is the only remaining position.

While these arguments have been defended at great length elsewhere (see Pereboom 2001, 2014, 2022; Caruso 2012, 2021a; Pereboom and Caruso 2018; Caruso and Pereboom 2022), I will briefly outline them in the following section. I will also examine which aspects admit of empirical considerations and which do not, in hopes of better understanding what neuroscience can and cannot answer and where philosophy must enter the picture.

4.4.1 Against Libertarianism

Libertarian accounts of free will can be divided into two general categories. According to *event-causal libertarianism,* actions are caused solely by events, and some type of indeterminacy in the production of actions by appropriate events is held to be a decisive requirement for moral responsibility (Kane 1996; Balaguer 2009; Lemos 2018). According to *agent-causal libertarianism,* on the other hand, free will of the sort required for moral responsibility is accounted for by the existence of agents who possess a causal power to make choices without being causally determined to do so (Taylor 1974; Chisholm 1976; O'Connor 2000; Clarke 2003). On this view, it is essential that the causation involved in an agent's making a free choice is not reducible to causation among events involving the agent – that is, it must irreducibly be an instance of the *agent-as-substance* causing a choice not by way of events.

Against event-causal libertarianism, I maintain that if actions are undetermined in the way the theory proposes, then agents lack the kind of control in action necessary to secure moral responsibility for them (see Pereboom 2001, 2014, 2021; Caruso 2012, 2021a). To be morally responsible in the basic desert sense for an action, it's necessary that the agent have a certain robust kind of control in acting. But on the event-causal libertarian account, only events are causes, and free decisions are causally undetermined. The causally relevant events antecedent to a decision – most prominently agent-involving events – accordingly leave it open whether the decision occurs, and thus do not *settle* whether it occurs. Settling whether a decision occurs is a kind of control in action, and the event-causal libertarian is a causalist about control, specifying that control in action is a causal matter. But because on this view all causation is event-causation, the agent can have no role in settling whether a decision occurs beyond the role it plays in agent-involving events. Because the agent "disappears" at the critical point in the production of the action—at the point at which whether it occurs is to be settled – Pereboom has called this the *disappearing agent argument* (2014).

While the disappearing agent objection provides sufficient reason on its own for rejecting event-causal libertarianism, it's also worth noting that the view posits several highly speculative and empirically unsupported assumptions that are unlikely to all be true. For instance, on Robert Kane's (1996) event-causal account, which is one of the most sophisticated and widely discussed, when we are confronted with difficult moral decisions and are torn as to what to do, this is "reflected in appropriate regions of our brains by movement away from thermo-dynamic equilibrium – in short, a kind of stirring up of chaos in the brain that makes it sensitive to micro-indeterminacies at the neuronal level" (2002: 417). Kane further proposes that these chaotic conditions amplify quantum indeter-minacy so that its effects "percolate up" to the "level of neural networks" (1996: 128–130). Lastly, Kane claims that, "when either of the [neural] pathways 'wins' (that is, reaches an activation threshold)," this amounts to a genuine example of choice (2002: 419).

Note, though, that:

> If multiple mutually exclusive aims did not cause the brain to go into a chaotic state the theory would be disproved. If it turned out that neurological systems weren't sensitive to quantum indeterminacies the theory would be disproved. If it turned out that neurological systems were sensitive to quantum indeter-minacies, but not sufficiently sensitive to amplify quantum indeterminacies in a way that affects the outcome of choice, this too would disprove the theory. These are not marginal or insubstantial bets about what brain science will reveal to us. (Vargas 2007: 143)

Similar empirical concerns apply to other leading event-causal accounts – including Mele (2006, 2017), Balaguer (2009), and Lemos (2018) – since they too posit indeterminacies at significantly high levels of brain processes. As a result, if quantum indeterminacy were shown not to exist at the appropriate neuronal level, then all these accounts would be empirically falsified. They would also be falsified if indeterminacy were not to exist at the right *temporal* moment in the proximate causal chain leading up to an agent deciding or making a choice, since each theory places the posited indeterminacy at some precise moment in the causal sequence.

Given the highly speculative nature of these empirical constraints and the current lack of empirical support for them, I contend that not only do event-causal accounts fail to preserve the control in action required for basic desert moral responsibility (a sufficient strike against them), but we also have good empirical reasons for being skeptical of such accounts. In fact, even proponents of these accounts acknowledge that we currently lack empirical evidence that human brains work as these theories demand (see Mele, 2017: 205; Lemos 2018: 6). This is problematic, especially when such assumptions are used to justify retributive legal punishment.

Turning now to agent-causal libertarianism, we can ask whether it fares any better. I contend that it does not. Common to all agent-causal accounts is the belief that an intelligible notion of an agent's causing an event can be given, according to which the kind of causation involved is fundamentally distinct from the kind that obtains between events. Agent-causal theorists introduce a new type of causation, *agent-causation*, to account for human agency and freedom. According to this notion of agent-causation, it is the agent him– or herself that causes, or initiates, free actions. And the agent, which is the cause of their own free actions, is a *self-determining* being, causally undetermined by antecedent events and conditions. The following passage by Roderick Chisholm does a good job of summing up the basic position:

> If we are responsible, and if what I have been trying to say [about agent causation] is true, then we have a prerogative which some would attribute only to God: each of us, when we act, is a prime unmoved mover. In doing what we do, we cause certain events to happen and nothing—or no one— causes us to cause those events to happen. (1964: 32)

O'Connor prefers the expression "not wholly moved movers" (2000: 67), but the point is similar: According to agent-causal accounts, the agent (qua substance) must be the cause of their decision or action but themselves not causally necessitated to perform just that action —that is, the agent must be a kind of uncaused cause.

There are, however, at least two fundamental problems with such accounts. The first is that the more the brain sciences progress and the better we understand the mechanisms that undergird human behavior, the more it becomes obvious that we lack what Tom Clark (2013) calls "soul control." There is no longer any reason to believe in a nonphysical self that controls action and is liberated from the physical laws of nature – a little *uncaused causer* capable of exercising counter-causal free will and creating *ex nihilo*. In fact, every day in every way, the behavioral, cognitive, and neurosciences eliminate the need to posit a libertarian soul/self/agent (qua substance) along with any serious work it might do. We must recognize that the metaphysical commitments of agent-causation are extremely demanding, at odds with our best philosophical and scientific theories about the world, and lack any independent justification. This is a significant, if not devastating, strike against it.

Second, *even if* one were willing to accept these metaphysical commitments, agent-causation would still need to be reconciled with the law-governing physical world for it to be taken seriously. Pereboom (2001, 2014), however, has argued that this cannot be done. Suppose that science reveals that the physical world is wholly governed by deterministic laws. Given this supposition, agent-causal libertarians may make room for their view by claiming that we agents are nonphysical beings and that this allows us to have the agent-causal power in an otherwise deterministic physical world. But this picture gives rise to a problem. On the path to a bodily movement resulting from an undetermined agent-caused decision, physical changes, for example, occur in the agent's brain. At this point, we would expect to encounter divergences from the deterministic laws. Alterations in the brain that result from the causally undetermined decision would themselves not be causally determined and would not be governed by deterministic laws. The agent-causalist may propose that the physical alterations that result from free decisions just happen to dovetail with what can be predicted on the basis of the deterministic laws, and then no event would occur that diverges from these laws. But this proposal features coincidences too wild to be credible. It appears, then, that agent-causal libertarianism cannot be reconciled with the physical world's being governed by deterministic laws. And a very similar objection can be set out if the laws of physics are fundamentally probabilistic and not deterministic (see Pereboom 2014: 67).

Such considerations reveal that agent-causal libertarianism is unable to reconcile agent-causes acting at the macrolevel (decisions and actions) with the microlevel being causally closed under the statistical laws. Of course, agent-causal theorists could always suggest that free decisions do, in fact, result in divergences from what we would expect given current theories of the physical laws. The problem with this proposal, however, is that we currently have no evidence that such divergences actually occur. Hence, it appears that agent-causal libertarianism is not reconcilable with either deterministic or probabilistic laws of nature, and we have no evidence that divergences from these laws are to be found.[7]

For the foregoing reasons, I conclude that we have sound reasons for rejecting the two leading forms of libertarian free will.

4.4.2 Against Compatibilism

The philosophical case for hard incompatibilism also requires arguing that the kind of free will necessary for basic desert moral responsibility is incompatible with the causal determination of action by natural factors beyond the agent's control. However, unlike the arguments against libertarianism – especially those that focused on empirical concerns – the case against compatibilism is primarily philosophical. *Compatibilism* maintains that even if all of our actions are causally determined by factors beyond our control, we can still have the kind of free will required to be morally responsible in the basic desert sense for them. Compatibilists of this kind point out that causal determination is irrelevant to the common criteria we use to ascertain whether people are blameworthy. Instead, compatibilists set out conditions for moral responsibility that do not require the

---

[7] A third objection, which I have discussed elsewhere but will leave aside here for the sake of space, is that agent-causal libertarianism also founders over the problem of mental causation (see Caruso 2012, 2021a).

falsity of determinism, and they argue that satisfying such compatibilist conditions is sufficient for responsibility.

While there are a number of powerful arguments against the compatibilist option – including the consequence argument (van Inwagen 1993), the basic argument (Strawson 1986, 1994), the no-forking paths argument (Fischer 1994), and the luck pincer (Levy 2011) – my preferred argument against compatibilism begins with the intuition that if an agent is causally determined to act by, for example, neuroscientists who unbeknownst to them manipulate their brain by optogenetic stimulation, then the agent will not be morally responsible for that action (in the basic desert sense) even if all the compatibilist conditions are met. The argument then continues and maintains that there is no relevant difference between such manipulated agents and their naturally determined counterparts that can justify the claim that manipulated agents are not morally responsible while determined agents are. Hence, if agents are not free and morally responsible in the basic desert sense under conditions of manipulation, then they are also not free and morally responsible in conditions of ordinary determinism. Such *manipulation arguments* therefore aim to show that an agent is not morally responsible in the basic desert sense if they are causally determined to act by factors beyond their control even if they satisfy all the compatibilist conditions (see Taylor 1974; Kane 1996; Pereboom 1995, 2001, 2014; Mele 2006).

While compatibilists have offered a number of replies to this argument, I contend that they all face significant objections (see Pereboom 2001, 2014, 2021; Caruso 2021a; Caruso in Dennett and Caruso 2021). I therefore conclude that determinism is incompatible with an agent being the appropriate source of their actions or controlling them in the right kind of way. This conclusion is a form of *source incompatibilism*, which maintains that an action is free in the sense required for moral responsibility only if it is not produced by a deterministic process that traces back to causal factors beyond the agent's control. Once we combine this conclusion with the conclusions of the previous sections – that is, that event-causal and agent-causal libertarian accounts of free will also fail to preserve the control in action required for basic desert moral responsibility – we see that hard incompatibilism is the only reasonable position to adopt.

4.5 The Epistemic Argument

If what I've argued in the previous sections is correct, we have sufficient reason for adopting the skeptical conclusion that who we are and what we do is ultimately the result of factors beyond our control (whether those factors be deterministic or indeterministic), and because of this, we are never morally responsible for our actions in the basic desert sense. Adopting this conclusion entails that retributivism is unjustified, and major revisions to the law are required. Furthermore, this argument in no way appeals to controversial claims about the timing of conscious will or presupposes the truth of determinism – hence, it differs significantly from the kind of neuroscientific argument against free will discussed earlier. It also differs from the kind of argument provided by Greene and Cohen (2004), since their argument relies heavily on intuitions about neurobiological determinism and the assumption that the criminal law is committed to an untenable libertarian account of agency. The hard incompatibilist argument for revision relies on neither of these things. Instead, it contends that *whether or not the law assumes a libertarian or compatibilist notion of free will*, it nonetheless is in need of revision – since there are powerful and insurmountable arguments against *both* kinds of free will, and neither is able to preserve the control in action required for basic desert moral responsibility and retributive punishment.

But what if one is still not convinced by the arguments for hard incompatibilism? Well, I maintain that *even in the face of uncertainty about the existence of free will*, it remains unclear whether retributive punishment is justified. This is because the burden of proof lies on those who want to inflict harm on others to provide good justification for such harm. This means that retributivists who want to justify legal punishment on the assumption that agents are free and morally responsible (and hence *justly deserve* to suffer for the wrongs they have done) must justify that assumption. And they must justify that assumption in a way that meets a high epistemic standard of proof since the harms caused in the case of legal punishment are often quite severe. It is not enough to simply point to the mere possibility that agents possess libertarian or compatibilist free will. Nor is it enough to say that the skeptical arguments against free will and basic desert moral responsibility fail to be conclusive. Rather, a positive and convincing case must be made that agents *are in fact* morally responsible in the basic desert sense, since it is the backward-looking desert of agents that retributivists take to justify the harm caused by legal punishment.

I call this second argument against retributive legal punishment the *Epistemic Argument* (Caruso 2020a, 2021a), and it can be summarized as follows:[8]

1. Legal punishment intentionally inflicts harms on individuals and the justification for such harms must meet a high epistemic standard. If it is significantly probable that one's justification for harming another is unsound, then, prima facie, that behavior is seriously wrong.

---

[8] Others who have defended similar arguments include Pereboom (2001), Vilhauer (2009, 2012), Shaw (2014), Corrado (2017), and Jeppsson (2021).

2. The retributive justification for legal punishment assumes that agents are morally responsible in the basic desert sense and hence justly deserve to suffer for the wrongs they have done in a backward-looking, non-consequentialist sense (appropriately qualified and under the constraint of proportionality).

3. If the justification for the assumption that agents are morally responsible in the basic desert sense, and hence justly deserve to suffer for the wrongs they have done, does not meet the high epistemic standard specified in (1), then retributive legal punishment is prima facie seriously wrong.

4. The justification for the claim that agents are morally responsible in the basic desert sense, provided by both libertarians and compatibilists, faces powerful and unresolved objections. As a result, it falls far short of the high epistemic bar needed to justify such harms.

5. Hence, retributive legal punishment is unjustified, and the harms it causes are prima facie seriously wrong.

Note that the Epistemic Argument requires only a weaker notion of skepticism than the one defended in the previous section, namely one that holds that the justification for believing that agents are morally responsible in the basic desert sense is *too weak* to justify the intentional suffering caused by retributive legal punishment. Unlike the arguments for hard incompatibilism, which aim to establish that no one is ever morally responsible for their actions in the basic desert sense, the Epistemic Argument does not require the refutation of libertarian and compatibilist accounts of free will. Instead, it simply needs to raise sufficient doubt that they succeed. And such doubt, I claim, is easy to raise. As a result, we should conclude that retributive legal punishment is unjustified and the harms it causes are prima facie seriously wrong (see Caruso 2021a for more details).

4.6 Revision

If we come to doubt or deny the existence of free will, or reject retributivism for other reasons, where does that leave us with regard to criminal justice? Well, traditionally, in addition to pure retributivism, there have been a number of other common justifications for legal punishment. Greene and Cohen, for instance, write: "There are perfectly good, forward-looking justifications for punishing criminals that do not depend on metaphysical fictions" (2004: 1783). Consequentialist deterrence theories have probably been the most discussed of these forward-looking alternatives. These theories maintain that we should only punish wrongdoers when it is rational to expect that it would maximize utility or consequentialist value relative to all the other options. These future benefits primarily include deterrence and increased safety. And the capacity to deter can further be divided into two different types: *general deterrence* and *specific* (or *special*) *deterrence*. General deterrence can be defined as the deterrence achieved from the threat of legal punishment on the public at large. Specific, or special, deterrence is deterrence aimed at previous offenders in order to reduce the likelihood of their re-offending.

While consequentialist theories are completely compatible with free will skepticism, some critics have argued that they suffer from their own independent moral difficulties (see Boonin 2008; Zimmerman 2011; Pereboom 2014; Caruso 2021a). First, critics object that deterrence theories have the potential to justify punishments that are intuitively too severe. This is because, in certain cases, harsh punishments would be more effective deterrents than milder forms. Second, such accounts could potentially justify punishing the innocent. Pereboom provides the following example: "If after a series of horrible crimes the actual perpetrator is not caught, potential criminals might come to believe that they can get away with serious wrongdoing. Under such circumstances it might maximize utility to frame and punish an innocent person" (2014: 164). Lastly, there is the "use" objection, which is a problem for consequentialism more generally – that is, consequentialism "sometimes requires people to be harmed severely, without their consent, in order to benefit others, and this is often intuitively wrong" (Pereboom 2014: 165). While some theorists think consequentialist deterrence theories can overcome these ethical concerns (see Greene and Cohen 2004; Bennett 2023), I prefer to avoid them by adopting an altogether different approach.

I maintain that there is an ethically defensible and practically workable alternative for dealing with dangerous crime that is not undercut by either free will skepticism or by other moral considerations. It is the *public health-quarantine model* developed and defended by me and Derk Pereboom (Pereboom 2001, 2014, 2021; Caruso 2016, 2017, 2021a, 2021b; Pereboom and Caruso 2018; Caruso and Pereboom 2020). The core idea of the model is that the right to harm in self-defense and defense of others justifies incapacitating the criminally dangerous with the minimum harm required for adequate protection. The theory is based on an analogy with quarantine and draws on a comparison between the treatment of dangerous criminals and the treatment of carriers of dangerous diseases. In its simplest form, it can be stated as follows: (1) Free will and basic desert skepticism maintain that criminals are not morally responsible for their actions in the basic desert sense; (2) plainly, many carriers of dangerous diseases are not responsible in this or in any other sense for having contracted these diseases; (3) yet, we generally agree that it is sometimes permissible to quarantine them, and the justification for doing so is the right to self-protection and the prevention of harm to others; (4) for similar reasons, even if a dangerous criminal is not morally responsible for his crimes in the basic desert sense (perhaps because no one is ever in this way morally responsible) it could be as legitimate to preventatively detain him as to quarantine the non-responsible carrier of a dangerous disease.

The first thing to note about the theory is that although one might justify quarantine (in the case of disease) and incapacitation (in the case of dangerous criminals) on purely utilitarian or consequentialist grounds, Pereboom and I resist this strategy. Instead, we maintain that incapacitation of the seriously dangerous is justified on the ground of the right to harm in self-defense and defense of others. That we have this right has broad appeal, much broader than utilitarianism or consequentialism more generally has. In addition, this makes the view more resilient to a number of objections and provides a more robust proposal for justifying criminal sanctions than other non-retributive options (Caruso 2021a, 2021b). One advantage it has, say, over consequentialist deterrence theories, is that it has more restrictions placed on it with regard to using people merely as a means. For instance, as it is illegitimate to treat carriers of a disease more harmfully than is necessary to neutralize the danger they pose, treating those with violent criminal tendencies more harshly than is required to protect society will be illegitimate as well. In fact, the model requires that we adopt the *principle of least infringement*, which holds that the least restrictive measures should be taken to protect public health and safety. This ensures that criminal sanctions will be proportionate to the danger posed by an individual, and any sanctions that exceed this upper bound will be unjustified.

Second, the quarantine model places several constraints on the treatment of criminals. First, as less dangerous diseases justify only preventative measures less restrictive than quarantine, so less dangerous criminal tendencies justify only more moderate restraints. We do not, for instance, quarantine people for the common cold, even though it has the potential to cause you some harm. Rather, we restrict the use of quarantine to a narrowly prescribed set of cases. Analogously, on this model, the use of incapacitation should be limited to only those cases where offenders are a serious threat to public safety and no less restrictive measures were available. In fact, for certain minor crimes, perhaps only some degree of monitoring could be defended. Second, the incapacitation account that results from this analogy demands a degree of concern for the rehabilitation and well-being of the criminal that would alter much of current practice. Just as fairness recommends that we seek to cure the diseased we quarantine, so fairness would counsel that we attempt to rehabilitate the criminals we detain. Rehabilitation and reintegration would therefore replace punishment as the focus of the criminal justice system. Lastly, if a criminal cannot be rehabilitated and our safety requires his indefinite confinement, this account provides no justification for making his life more miserable than would be required to guard against the danger he poses.

In addition to these restrictions on harsh and unnecessary treatment, the model also advocates for a broader approach to criminal behavior that moves beyond the narrow focus on sanctions. Most importantly, it situates the quarantine analogy within the broader justificatory framework of public health ethics (Caruso 2016, 2021a). Public health ethics not only justifies quarantining carriers of dangerous diseases on the grounds that it is necessary to protect public health, but it also requires that we take active steps to prevent such outbreaks from occurring in the first place. The analogous claim holds for incapacitation. Taking a public health approach to criminal behavior allows us to justify the incapacitation of dangerous criminals when needed, but it also makes prevention a primary function of the criminal justice system. So instead of focusing on punishment, the public health-quarantine model shifts the focus to identifying and addressing the systemic causes of crime, such as poverty, low socioeconomic status, systematic disadvantage, mental illness, homelessness, educational inequity, exposure to abuse and violence, poor environmental health, and addiction.

In fact, the public health framework sees *social justice* as a foundational cornerstone to public health and safety (Caruso 2021b). In public health ethics, a failure on the part of public health institutions to ensure the social conditions necessary to achieve a sufficient level of health is considered a grave injustice. An important task of public health ethics, then, is to identify which inequalities in health are the most egregious and thus which should be given the highest priority in public health policy and practice. The public health approach to criminal behavior likewise maintains that a core moral function of the criminal justice system is to identify and remedy social and economic inequalities responsible for crime. Just as public health is negatively affected by poverty, racism, and systemic inequality, so too is public safety. This broader approach to criminal justice therefore places issues of social justice at the forefront. It sees racism, sexism, poverty, and systemic disadvantage as serious threats to public safety and prioritizes the reduction of such inequalities.

Summarizing the public health-quarantine model, then, the core idea is that the right to harm in self-defense and defense of others justifies incapacitating the criminally dangerous with the minimum harm required for adequate protection. The resulting account would not justify the sort of criminal punishment whose legitimacy is most dubious, such as death or confinement in the common kinds of prisons in the United States. The model also specifies attention to the well-being of criminals, which would change much of the current policy. Furthermore, the public health component of the theory prioritizes prevention and social justice and aims to identify and take action on the social determinants of health and criminal behavior. This combined approach to dealing with criminal behavior, I maintain, is sufficient for dealing with dangerous criminals, leads to a more humane and effective social policy, and is actually preferable to the harsh and often excessive forms of punishment that typically come with retributivism.

References

Abrams, Z. (2022). The psychological science of adolescent behavior and decision-making is reshaping the juvenile justice system. *Monitoring on Psychology* 53(8): 48.

Aharoni, E., S. Abdulla, C. H. Allen, and T. Nagelhoffer. (2022). Ethical implications of neurobiologically informed risk assessment for criminal justice decisions: A case for pragmatism. In *Neuroscience and Philosophy*, eds. F. De Brigard and W. Sinnott-Armstrong, pp.161–193. Cambridge, MA: MIT Press.

Aharoni, E., J. Mallett, G. M. Vincent, et al. (2014). Predictive accuracy in the neuroprediction of rearrest. *Social Neuroscience* 9(4): 332–336.

Aharoni, E., G. M. Vincent, C. L. Harenski, et al. (2013). Neuroprediction of future rearrest. *Proceedings of the National Academy of Sciences of the United States of America* 110(15): 6223–6228.

Alces, P. A. (2018). *The Moral Conflict of Law and Neuroscience*. Chicago: University of Chicago Press.

American Psychological Association. (2004). The polygraph in doubt: Because of the nature of deception, there is no good wat to validate the test for making judgments about criminal behavior. *Monitor on Psychology* 35(7): 71.

American Society for Addiction Medicine. (2017). *Advancing Access to Addiction Medications*. https://nosorh.org/wp-content/uploads/2017/05/Access-to-MAT-by-state.pdf.

Anderson, N. E., and K. A. Kiehl. (2014). Psychopathy: Developmental perspectives and their implications for treatment. *Restorative Neurology Neuroscience* 32(1): 103–117.

Aono, D., G. Yaffe, and H. Kober. (2019). Neuroscientific evidence in the courtroom: A review. *Cognitive Research: Principles and Implications* 4(4): 1–20.

Aspinwall, L. G., T. R. Brown, and J. Tabery. (2012). The double-edged sword: Does biomechanism increase or decrease judges' sentencing of psychopaths? *Science* 337: 846–849.

Balaguer, M. (2009). *Free Will as an Open Scientific Problem*. Boston: MIT Press.

Barrow, R. L., and H. D. Fabing. (1956). *Epilepsy and Law: A Proposal for Legal Reform in the Light of Medical Progress*. New York: Hoeber-Harper.

Bennett, C. (2023). Rethinking four criticisms of consequentialist theories of punishment. In *The Palgrave Handbook on the Philosophy of Punishment*, ed. M. C. Altman, pp.171–194. New York: Palgrave Macmillian.

Bjornsson, G., and D. Pereboom. (2014). Free will skepticism and bypassing. In *Moral Psychology: Vol. 4*, ed. W. Sinnott-Armstrong, pp. 142–157. Cambridge, MA: MIT Press.

Blair, R. J. R., and L. Cipolotti. (2000). Impaired social response reversal: A case of acquired sociopathy. *Brain* 123: 1122–41.

Boggio, P. S., A. B. Villani, S. Zaghi, et al. (2010). Modulation of risk-taking in marijuana users by transcranial direct current stimulation (tDCS) of the dorsolateral prefrontal cortex. *Drug and Alcohol Dependency* 112(3): 220–225.

Bohm, D. (1952). A suggested interpretation of quantum theory in terms of "hibbed" variables, I and II. *Physics Review* 85(2): 166–193.

Bomann-Larsen, L. (2011). Voluntary rehabilitation? On neurotechnological behavioral treatment, valid consent and (in)appropriate offers. *Neuroethics* 6(1): 65–77.

Boonin, D. (2008). *The Problem of Punishment*. New York: Cambridge University Press.

Burns, J. M., and R. H. Swerdlow. (2003). Right orbitofrontal tumor with pedophilia systmptom and constructional apraxia sign. *Archives of Neurology* 60(3): 437–440.

Caplan, A. (2006). Ethical issues surrounding forced, mandated, or coerced treatment. *Journal of Substance Abuse Treatment* 31(2): 117–120.

Caruso, G. D. (2012). *Free Will and Consciousness: A Determinist Account of the Illusion of Free Will*. Lanham, MD: Lexington Boos.

Caruso, G. D. (2016). Free will skepticism and criminal behavior: A public health-quarantine model. *Southwestern Philosophical Review* 32(1): 25–48.

Caruso, G. D. (2017). *Public Health and Safety: The Social Determinants of Health and Criminal Behavior*. London: ResearchLinks Books.

Caruso, G. D. (2018). Skepticism about moral responsibility. *Stanford Encyclopedia of Philosophy*. https://plato.stanford.edu/entries/skepticism-moral-responsibility/.

Caruso, G. D. (2020a). Justice without retribution: An epistemic argument against retributive criminal punishment. *Neuroethics* 13(1): 13–28.

Caruso, G. D. (2020b). Abolish the case bail system. *Arc Digital*, October 9. https://medium.com/arc-digital/abolish-the-cash-bail-system-3cf6476ecaae

Caruso, G. D. (2021a). *Rejecting Retributivism: Free Will, Punishment, and Criminal Justice*. New York: Cambridge University Press.

Caruso, G. D. (2021b). Retributivism, free will skepticism, and the public health-quarantine model: Replies to Kennedy, Walen, Corrado, Sifferd, Pereboom, and Shaw. *Journal of Legal Philosophy* 46(2): 161–216.

Caruso, G. D., and S. G. Morris. (2017). Compatibilism and retributive desert moral responsibility: On what is of central philosophical and practical importance. *Erkenntnis* 82: 837–855.

Caruso, G. D., and D. Pereboom. (2020). A non-punitive alternative to punishment. In *Routledge Handbook of the Philosophy and Science of Punishment*, eds. F. Focquaert, B. Waller, and E. Shaw, pp. 355–365. New York: Routledge.

Caruso, G. D., and D. Pereboom. (2022). *Reconsidering Moral Responsibility*. New York: Cambridge University Press.

Caruso, J. P., and J. P. Sheehan. (2017). Psychosurgery, ethics, and media: A history of Walter Freeman and lobotomy. *Neurosurgical Focus* 43(3): 1–8.

Castelli, L., P. Perozzo, M. Zibetti, et al. (2006). Chronic deep brain stimulation of the subthalamic nucleus for Parkinson's disease: Effects on cognition, mood, anxiety, and personality traits. *European Neurology* 55: 136–144.

Castelli L., P. Perozzo, M. Caglio, et al. (2008). Does subthalamic nucleus for Parkinson's disease: Effects on cognition, mood, anxiety, and personality traits. *European Neurology* 55: 136–144.

Chisholm, R. (1964). Human freedom and the self. *The Lindley Lecture*. Reprinted in *Free Will*, ed. G. Watson, pp. 24–35. New York: Oxford University Press.

Chisholm, R. (1976). *Person and Object: A Metaphysic Study*. La Salle: Open Court.

Choy. O., F. Focquaert, and A. Raine. (2020). Benign biological interventions to reduce offending. *Neuroethics* 13(1): 29–41.

Choy, O., A. Raine, and R. H. Hamilton. (2018). Stimulation of the prefrontal cortex reduces intentions to commit aggression: A randomized, double-blind, placebo- controlled, stratified, parallel-group trial. *Journal of Neuroscience* 38(29): 6505–6512.

Clarke, R. (2003). *Libertarian Accounts of Free Will*. New York: Oxford Unversity Press.

Clark, T. (2013). Clark comments on Dennett's review of Against Moral Responsibility, Naturalism.org: www.naturalism.org/resources/book-reviews/exchange-on-wallers-against-moral-responsibility.

Cornell, D. G., J. Warren, G. Hawk, E. Staffoed, G. Oram, and D. Pine. (1996). Psychopathy in instrumental and reactive violent offenders. *Journal of Consulting and Clinical Psychology* 64(4): 783–790.

Corrado, M. (2017). Punishment and the burden of proof. UNC Legal Studies Research Paper. SRRN: https://ssrn.com/abstract=2997654 or https://doi .org/10.2139/ssrn.2997654.

Dalkner, N., H. F. Unterrainer, G. Wood, et al. (2017). Short-term beneficial effects of 12 sessions of neurofeedback on avoidant personality accentuation in the treatment of alcohol use disorder. *Frontiers of Psychology* 8: 1688.

Darby, R. R., A. Horn, F. Cushman, and M. D. Fox. (2017). Lesion network localization of criminal behavior. *PNAS* 115(3): 601–606.

Davatzikos, C., K. Ruparel, Y. Fan, et al. (2005). Classifying spatial patterns of brain activity with machine learning methods: Application to lie detection. *NeuroImage* 28: 663–668.

Delfin, C., H. Krona, P. Andiné, et al. (2019). Prediction of recidivism in a long-term follow-up of forensic psychiatric patients: Incremental effects of neuroimaging data. *PLoS One* 14(5): e0217127.

Dennett, D. C., and G. D. Caruso. (2021). *Just Deserts: Debating Free Will*. New York: Polity.

Denno, D. W. (2015). The myth of the double-edged sword: An empirical study of neuroscience evidence in criminal cases. *Boston College Law Review* 56(2): 493–551.

De Oliveira-Souza, R., R. D. Hare, I. E. Bramati, et al. (2008). Psychopathy as a disorder of the moral brain: Fronto temporo-limbic gray matter reductions demonstrated by vox-based morphometry. *Neuroimage* 40(3): 1202–1213.

Douglas, T. (2014a). Criminal rehabilitation though medical intervention: Moral liability and the right to bodily integrity. *Journal of Ethics* 18: 101–119.

Douglas, T. (2014b). Blurred lines: Neurointerventions in crime prevention. *The University of Otago Magazine*. www.otago.ac.nz/otagomagazine/issue39/profiles/otago080465.html.

Douglas, T. (2019). Nonconsensual neurocorrectives and bodily integrity: A reply to Shaw and Barn. *Journal of Ethics* 12: 107.

Douglas, T., P. Bonte, F. Focquart, K. Devolder, and S. Sterckx. (2013). Coercion, incarceration, and chemical castration: An argument from autonomy. *Journal of Bioethical Inquiry* 10(3): 393–405.

Douglas, T., J. Pugh, I. Singh, J. Savulescu, and S. Fazel. (2017). Risk assessment tools in criminal justice and forensic psychiatry: The need for better data. *European Psychiatry: The Journal of the Association of European Psychiatrists* 42: 134–137.

Du, Y. (2020). The application of neuroscience evidence on court sentencing decisions: Suggesting guideline for neuro-evidence. *Seattle Journal for Social Justice* 19(2): 493–523.

Ermer, E., L. M. Cope, P. K. Nyalakanti, V. D. Calhoun, and K. A. Kiehl. (2011). Aberrant paralimbic gray matter in criminal psychopathy. *Journal of Abnormal Psychology* 121(3): 649–658.

Farahany, N.A. (2016). Neuroscience and behavioral genetics in US criminal law: An empirical analysis. *Journal of Law and Biosciences* 2(3): 485–509.

Farahany, N. A. (2023). *The Battle for Your Brain: Defending Your Right to Think Freely in the Age of Neurotechnology*. New York: St. Martin Press, MacMillan.

Fecteau, S., D. Knoch, F. Fregni, et al. (2007). Diminished risk-taking behavior by modulating activity in the prefrontal cortex: A direct current stimulation study. *Journal of Neuroscience* 27(46): 12500–12505.

Fedoroff, J. P., R. Wisner-Carlson, S. Dean, and F. S. Berlin. (1992). Medroxy-progesterone acetate in the treatment of paraphilic sexual disorders: Rate of relapse in paraphilic men treated in long-term group psychotherapy with or without medroxy-progesterone acetate. *Journal of Offender Rehabilitation* 18(3–4): 109–123.

Fischer, J. M. (1994). *The Metaphysics of Free Will: An Essay on Control*. Oxford: Blackwell.

Focquaert, F. (2014). Mandatory neurotechnological treatment: Ethical issues. *Theoretical Medicine and Bioethics* 35: 59–72.

Focquaert, F., and D. DeRidder. (2009). Direct intervention in the brain: Ethical issues concerning personal identity. *Journal of Ethics in Mental Health* 4(2): 1–7.

Focquaert, F., and M. C. Erasmus. (2015). Moral enhancement: Do means matter morally. *Neuroethics* 8: 139–151.

Focquaert, F., A. L. Glenn, and A. Raine. (2013). Free will, responsibility, and the punishment of criminals. In *The Future of Punishment*, ed. T. A. Nadelhoffer, pp. 247–274. New York: Oxford University Press.

Focquaert, F., K. Van Assche, and S. Sterckx. (2020). Offering neurointerventions to offenders with cognitive-emotional impairments: Ethical and criminal justice aspects. In *Neurointerventions and the Law*, eds. N. A. Vincent, T. Nadelhoffer, and A. McCay, pp.127–148. New York: Oxford University Press.

Forsberg, L., and T. Douglas. (2017). Anti-libidinal interventions in sex offenders: Medical or correctional? *Medical Law Review* 24(4): 453–473.

Gamer, M. (2014). Mind reading using neuroimaging: Is this the future of deception detection? *European Psychologist* 19(3): 172–183.

Ganis, G., S. M. Kosslyn, S. Stose, W. L. Thompson, and D. A. Yurgelum-Todd. (2011). Lying in the scanner: Covert countermeasures disrupt deception detection by functional magnetic resonance imaging. *NeuroImage* 55: 312–319.

Gkotsi, G. M., and L. Benaroyo. (2012). Criminal offenders: Some ethical issues. *Journal of Ethics in Mental Health* 6: 1–7.

Glannon, W. (2007). *Bioethics and the Brain*. New York: Oxford University Press.

Glenn, A. L., A. Raine, P. S. Yaralian, and Y. Yang. (2010). Increased volume of the striatum in psychopathic individuals. *Biological Psychiatry* 67: 52–58.

Glenn, A. L., Y. Yang, and A. Raine. (2012). Neuroimaging in psychopathy and antisocial personality disorder: Functional significance and neurodevelopmental hypothesis. In *Neuroimaging in Forensic Psychiatry: From the Clinical to the Courtroom*, ed. J. R. Simpson, pp.81–98. Oxford: Wiley-Blackwell.

Grafton, S., W. Sinnott-Armstrong, S. Gazzaniga, and M. Gazzaniga. (2006). Brain scans go legal. *Scientific American* 17: 30–37.

Greely, H. T. (2007). Neuroscience and criminal justice: Not responsibility but treatment. *University of Kansas Law Review* 56(5): 1103–1138.

Greely, H. T. (2013). Neuroscience, mindreading, and the law. In *A Primer on Criminal Law and Neuroscience*, eds. S. J. Morse and A. L. Roskies, pp. 120–149. New York: Oxford University Press.

Greely, H. T., and N. A. Farahany. (2019). Neuroscience and the criminal justice system. *Annual Review of Criminology* 2: 451–471.

Greely, H. T., and J. Illes. (2007). Neuroscience-based lie detection: The urgent need for regulation. *American Journal of Law and Medicine* 33: 377–431.

Green, E., and B. S. Cahill. (2012). Effects of neuroimaging evidence on mock juror decision making. *Behavioral Science and Law* 30(3): 280.

Green, J., and J. Cohen. (2004). For the law, neuroscience changes nothing and everything. *Philosophical transactions: Biological Sciences* 359(1451): 1775–1785.

Grove, W. M., and P. E. Meehl. (1996). Comparative efficiency of informal (subjective, impressionistic) and formal (mechanical, algorithmic) prediction procedures: The clinical-statistical controversy. *Psychology, Public Policy, and Law* 2(2): 293–323.

Grubin, D. (2018). The pharmacological treatment of sex offenders. In *The Wiley Blackwell Handbook of Forensic Neuroscience*, eds. A. R. Beech, A. J. Carter, R. E. Mann, and P. Rothstein, pp. 703–724. New York: Wiley-Blackwell.

Hamilton, M. (2021a). Investigating algorithmic risk and race. *UCLA Criminal Justice Law Review* 5(1): 53–102.

Hamilton, M. (2022b). Evaluating algorithmic risk assessment. *New Criminal Law Review* 24(2): 156–211.

Hare, R. D., and L. M. McPherson. (1984). Violent and aggressive behavior by criminal psychopaths. *International Journal of Law and Psychiatry* 7: 35–50.

Hemphill, J. F., R. D. Hare, and S. Wong. (1998). Psychopathy and recidivism: A review. *Legal Criminology and Psychology* 3(1): 139–170.

Hirstein, W., K. L. Sifferd, and T. K. Fagan. (2018). *Responsible Brains: Neuroscience, Law and Human Culpability*. New York: MIT Press.

Houeto, J.-L., L. Mallet, V. Mesnaga, et al. (2006). Subthalamic stimulation in Parkinson disease: Behavior and social adaption. *Archives of Neurology* 63: 1090–1095.

Hucker, S., R. Langevin, and J. Bain. (1988). A double blind trial of sex drive reducing medication in pedophiles. *Sexual Abuse: A Journal of Research and Treatment* 1(2): 227–242.

Jackson, J. (2009). Re-conceptualizing the right of silence as an effective fair trial standard. *International Comparable Law Quarterly* 58: 835–861.

Jeppsson, S. (2021). Retributivism, justification and credence: The epistemic argument revisited. *Neuroethics* 14(2): 177–190.

Kane, R. (1996). *The Significance of Free Will*. New York: Oxford University Press.

Kane, R. (2002). Some neglected pathways in the free will labyrinth. In *The Oxford Handbook of Free Will*, ed. R. Kane, pp.406–437. New York: Oxford University Press.

Kaplan, S. (2015). The execution of Ceil Clayton and the biology of blame. *The Washington Post*, March 18. www.washingtonpost.com/news/morning-mix/wp/2015/03/18/the-execution-of-cecil-clayton-and-the-biology-of-blame/.

Kiehl, K. A., N. E. Anderson, E. Aharoni, et al. (2018). Age of gray matters: Neuroprediction of recidivism. *NeuroImage: Clinical* 19: 813–823.

Kozel, F. A., K. A. Johnson, M. Qiwen, et al. (2005). Detecting deception using functional magnetic resonance imaging. *Biological Psychiatry* 58: 605–613.

Langleben, D. D., F. Dattilo, and T. Guthei. (2006). True lies: Delusions and lie-detection technology. *Journal of Psychiatry Law* 34: 351–370.

Laura and John Arnold Foundation. (2013). *Developing A Notional Model for Pretrial Risk Assessment*. https://craftmediabucket.s3.amazonaws.com/uploads/PDFs/LJAF-research-summary_PSA-Court_4_1.pdf.

Lemos, J. (2018). *A Pragmatic Approach to Libertarian Free Will*. New York: Routledge.

Leutgeb, V., M. Leitner, A. Wabnegger, et al. (2015). Brain abnormalities in high-risk violence offenders and their association with psychopathic traits and criminal recidivism. *Neuroscience* 12(308): 194–201.

Levy, N. (2005). Libet's impossible demand. *Journal of Consciousness Studies* 12(1): 67–76.

Levy, N. (2007). *Neuroethics: Challenges for the 21ˢᵗ Century*. New York: Cambridge University Press.

Levy, N. (2011). *Hard Luck: How Luck Undermines Free Will and Moral Responsibility*. New York: Oxford University Press.

Levy, N. (2012). Neuroethics. *WIREs Cognitive Science* 3: 143–151.

Lewis, P. T. (2016). *Quantum Ontology: A Guide to the Metaphysics of Quantum Mechanics*. New York: Oxford University Press.

Libet, B. (1985). Unconscious cerebral initiation and the role of conscious will in voluntary action. *Behavioral and Brain Science* 8: 529–566.

Libet, B. (1999). Do we have free will? *Journal of Consciousness Studies* 6(8–9): 47–57.

Libet, B., C. A. Gleason, E. W. Wright, and D. K. Pearl. (1983). Time of conscious intention to act in relation to onset of cerebral activity (readiness-potential): The unconscious initiation of a freely voluntary act. *Brain* 106: 623–642.

Maletzky, B. M., A. Tolan, and B. McFarland. (2006). The Oregon depo-provera program: A five-year follow-up. *Sexual Abuse: A Journal of Research and Treatment* 18(3): 303–316.

Martin, G., and C. L. Johnson. (2005). The boys totem town neurofeedback project: A pilot study of EEG biofeedback with incarcerated juvenile felons. *Journal of Neurotherapy* 9(3): 71–86.

McCay, A. (2022). Neurotechnology, law and the legal profession. *Horizon Report for the Law Society*, August: 1–29. www.scottishlegal.com/uploads/Neurotechnology-law-and-the-legal-profession-full-report-Aug-2022.pdf.

McGirr, A., F. Van den Eynde, E. Chachamovich, M. Fleck, M. Berlim. (2014). Personality dimensions and deep repetitive transcranial magnetic stimulations (DTMS) for treatment-resistant depression: A pilot trial on five-factor prediction of antidepressant response. *Neuroscience Letters* 563: 144–148.

Meixner, J. B. (2016). The use of neuroscience evidence in criminal proceedings. *Journal of Law and the Biosciences* 3(2): 330–335.

Mele, A. (2006). *Free Will and Luck*. New York: Oxford University Press.

Mele, A. (2009). *Effective Intentions*. New York: Oxford University Press.

Mele, A. (2017). *Aspects of Agency: Decisions, Abilities, Explanations, and Free Will*. New York: Oxford University Press.

Meyer, B., M. K. Byrne, C. H. Collier, et al. (2015). Baseline omega-3 index correlates with aggressive and attention deficit disorder behaviours in adult prisoners. *PLoS One* 10(3): e0120220.

Meynen, G. (2014). Neurolaw: Neuroscience, ethics, and law. *Ethical Theory and Moral Practice* 17: 819–829.

Morse, S. J. (2005). Brain overclaim syndrome and criminal responsibility: A diagnostic note. *Ohio State Journal of Criminal Law* 3: 397–412.

Morse, S. J. (2013). Common criminal law compatibilism. In *Neuroscience and Legal Responsibility*, ed. N. A. Vincent, pp. 27–52. New York: Oxford University Press.

Morse, S. J. (2015). Criminal law and common sense: An essay on the perils and promise of neuroscience. *Marquette Law Review* 99: 39–72.

Morse, S. J. (2018). The neuroscience non-challenge to meaning, morals, and purpose. In *Neuroexistentialism: Meaning, Morals, and Purpose in the Age of Neuroscience*, eds. G. D. Caruso and O. Flanagan, pp. 333–358. New York: Oxford University Press.

Morse, S. J., and A. L. Roskies. (eds.) (2013). *A Primer on Criminal Law and Neuroscience: A Contribution of the Law and Neuroscience Project.* New York: Oxford University Press.

Moser, D. J., S. Arndt, J. E. Kanz, et al. (2004). Coercion and informed consent in research involving prisoners. *Comprehensive Psychiatry* 45(1): 1–9.

Nadelhoffer, T., S. Bibas, S. Grafton, et al. (2012). Neuroprediction, violence, and the law: Setting the stage. *Neuroethics* 5(1): 67–99.

Nahmias, E. (2011). Intuitions about free will, determinism, and bypassing. In *The Oxford Handbook of Free Will, 2nd ed.*, ed. R. Kane, pp.555–576. New York: Oxford University Press.

National Institute of Drug Abuse. (2021). *Medications to Treat Opioid Use Disorder: Research Report.* https://nida.nih.gov/download/21349/medications-to-treat-opioid-use-disorder-research-report.pdf?v=99088f7584dac93ddcfa98648065bfbe.

O'Connor, T. (2000). *Persons and Causes.* New York: Oxford University Press.

Pardo, M. S., and D. Patterson. (2013). *Minds, Brains, and Law: The Conceptual Foundations of Law and Neuroscience.* New York: Oxford University Press.

Pereboom, D. (1995). Determinism al dente. *Nous* 29: 21–45.

Pereboom, D. (2001). *Living without Free Will.* New York: Cambridge University Press.

Pereboom, D. (2014). *Free Will, Agency, and Meaning in Life.* New York: Oxford University Press.

Pereboom, D. (2021). *Wrongdoing and the Moral Emotions.* New York: Oxford University Press.

Pereboom, D. (2022). *Free Will.* New York: Cambridge University Press.

Pereboom, D., and G. D. Caruso. (2018). Hard-incompatibilist existentialism: Neuroscience, punishment, and meaning in life. In *Neuroexistentialism: Meaning, Morals, and Purpose in the Age of Neuroscience*, eds. G. D. Caruso and O. Flanagan, pp.193–222. New York: Oxford University Press.

Philipp-Wiegmann, F., M. Rosler, K. D. Romer, et al. (2011). Reducing cortical inhibition in violent offenders: A study with transcranial magnetic stimulation. *Neuropsychobiology* 64(2): 86–92.

Porter, S., A. Birt, and D. P. Boer. (2001). Investigation of the criminal and conditional release profiles of Canadian federal offenders as a function of psychopathy and age. *Law and Human Behavior* 25(6): 647–661.

Porter, S., L. Brinke, and K. Wilson. (2009). Profiles and conditional release performance of psychopathic and non-psychopathic sexual offenders. *Legal Criminology and Psychology* 14(1): 109–111.

Poythress, N. G., J. Petrila, A. McGaha, and R. Boothroyd. (2002). Perceived coercion and procedural justice in the Broward mental health court. *International Journal of Law and Psychiatry* 25(5): 517–533.

Pugh, J., and T. Douglas. (2017). Neurointerventions as criminal rehabilitation: An ethical review. In *Routledge Handbook of Criminal Justice Ethics*, eds. J. Jacobs and J. Jackson, pp.95–109. New York: Routledge.

Quirk, D.A. (1995). Composite biofeedback conditioning and dangerous offenders. *Journal of Neurotherapy* 1(2): 44–54.

Raine, A. (2014). *The Anatomy of Violence: The Biological Roots of Crime.* New York: Vintage.

Raine, A., T. Lencz, S. Bihrle, L. LaCasse, and P. Colletti. (2000). Reduced prefrontal gray matter volume and reduced autonomic activity in antisocial personality disorder. *Archives of General Psychiatry* 57: 119–127.

Raine, A., J. H. Portnoy, J. H. Liu, T. Mahoomed, and J. R. Hibben. (2015). Reduction in the behavior problems with omga-3 supplements in children aged 8–16 years: A randomized, double-blind, placebo-controlled, stratified, parallel-group trial. *Journal of Child Psychology and Psychiatry* 56(5): 509–520.

Raymond, J., C. Varney, L. A. Parkinson, and J. H. Gruzelier. (2005). The effects of alpha/theta neurofeedback on personality and mood. *Cognitive Brain Research* 23: 287–282.

Redlich, A. D., S. Hoover, A. Summers, H. J. Steadman. (2010). Enrollment in mental health courts: Voluntariness, knowingness, and adjudicative competence. *Law and Human Behavior* 34(2): 91–104.

Rice, M. E., and G. T. Harris. (2003). The size and sign of treatment effects in sex offender therapy. *Sexually Coercive Behavior: Understanding and Management* 989: 428–440.

Rigg, J. (2002). Measures of perceived coercion in prison treatment settings. *International Journal of Law and Psychiatry* 25(5): 473–490.

Romero-Martinez, A., S. Bressanutti, and L. Moya-Albiol. (2020). A systematic review of the effectiveness of non-invasive brain stimulation techniques to reduce violence proneness by interfering in anger and irritability. *Journal of Clinical Medicine* 9(3): 882–903.

Ryberg, J. (2019). *Neurointerventions, Crime and Punishment: Ethical Considerations*. New York: Oxford University Press.

Roskies, A. (2002). Neuroethics for the new millennium. *Neuron* 35: 21–23.

Roskies, A. (2021). Neuroethics. *Stanford Encyclopedia of Philosophy*. Substantive revisions, March 3, 2021. https://plato.stanford.edu/entries/neuroethics/

Roth, M. (2018). *Philosophical Foundations of Neurolaw*. Lanham, Maryland: Lexington Books.

Rusconi, E., and T. Mitchener-Nissen. (2013). Prospects of functional magnetic resonance imaging as lie detector. *Frontiers in Human Neuroscience* 7: 1–12.

Rushing, S. E. (2014), The admissibility of brain scans in criminal trials: The case of positron emission tomography. *Court Review* 50: 62–69.

Ryberg, J. (2019). *Neurointerventions, Crime, and Punishment*. New York: Oxford University Press.

Sajous-Turner, A., N. E. Anderson, M. Widdows, et. al. (2020). Aberrant brain gray matter in murderers. *Brain Imaging and Behavior* 14(5): 2050–2061.

Salekin, R. T., R. Rogers, and K. W. Sewell. (1996). A review and meta-analysis of the psychopathy checklist and psychopathy checklist-revised: Predictive validity of dangerousness. *Clinical Psychological Sciences* 3(3): 203–215.

Shaw, E. (2014). *Free Will, Punishment, and Criminal Responsibility*. Dissertation Thesis. Edinburgh University.

Shaw, E. (2018a). Retributivism and the moral enhancement of criminals through brain interventions. *Royal Institute of Philosophy Supplement* 83: 251–270.

Shaw, E. (2018b). Against the mandatory use of neurointerventions in criminal sentencing. In *Treatment for Crime: Philosophical Essays on Neurointerventions in Criminal Justice*, eds. D. Birks and T. Douglas, pp. 321–337. New York: Oxford University Press.

Shaw, E. (2019). The right to bodily integrity and the rehabilitation of offenders through medical interventions: A reply to Thomas Douglas. *Neuroethics* 12: 97–106.

Shaw, E. (2022). Neuroscience, criminal sentencing, and human rights. *William and Mary Law Review* 63: 1409–1443.

Shen, F. X. (2016). The overlooked history of neurolaw. *Fordham Law Review* 85(2): 667–695.

Sifferd, K. L. (2020). Chemical castration as punishment. In *Neuro-Interventions and the Law*, eds. T. Nadelhoffer and N. A. Vincent, pp. 513–533. New York: Oxford University Press.

Simpson, J. (2008). Functional MRI lie detection: Too good to be true? *Journal of American Academy of Psychiatry Law* 36: 491–498.

Smith, P. N., and M. W. Sams. (2005). Neurofeedback with juvenile offenders: A pilot study in the use of QEEG-based and anlog-based remedial neurofeedback training. *Journal of Neurotherapy* 9(3): 97–99.

Soon, C. S., M. Brass, H.-J. Heinze, and J.-D. Haynes. (2008). Unconscious determinants of free decisions in the human brain. *Nature Neuroscience* 11(5): 543–545.

Steinberg, L., and E. S. Scott. (2003). Less guilty by reason of adolescence: Developmental immaturity, diminished responsibility, and the juvenile death penalty. *American Psychologist* 58(12): 1009–1018.

Straiton, J, and F. Lake. (2021). Inside the brain of a killer: The ethics of neuroimaging in a criminal conviction. *BioTechniques* 70(2): 69–71.

Strawson, G. (1986). *Freedom and Belief.* New York: Oxford University Press.

Strawson. G. (1994). The impossibility of moral responsibility. *Philosophical Studies* 75(1): 5–24.

Taylor, J. Sherrod, J. A. Harp, and T. Elliot. (1991). Neuropsychologists and neurolawyers. *Neuropsychology* 5(4): 293–305.

Taylor, R. (1974). *Metaphysics*, 4th ed. Englewood Cliffs, NJ: Prentice-Hall.

Taxman, F. S. (2018). The partially clothed emperor: Evidence-based practices. *Journal of Contemporary Criminal Justice* 34(97): 97–98.

Tiihonen, J., R. Rossi, M. Laakso, et al. (2008). Brain anatomy of persistent violent offenders: More rather than less. *Psychiatric Research and Neuroimaging* 163(3): 201–212.

To, W. T., J. Eroh, J. Hart, and S. Vanneste. (2018). Exploring the effects of anodal and cathodal high-definition transcranial direct current stimulation targeting the dorsal anterior cingulate cortex. *Scientific Reports* 8(1): 4454.

US Congress Office of Technology Assessment. (1983). *Scientific Validity of Polygraph Testing: A Research Review and Evaluation*. Washington, DC: US Congress, Office of Technology Assessment.

Vaidman, L. (2014). Quantum theory and determinism. *Quantum Studies: Mathematics and Foundations* 1: 5–38.

Van Inwagen, P. (1993). *An Essay on Free Will*. New York: Clarendon Press.

Vargas, M. (2007). Revision. In *Four Views on Free Will*, eds. J. M. Fischer, R. Kane, D. Pereboom, and M. Vargas, pp.126–165. Malden, MA: Blackwell.

Vilhauer, B. (2009). Free will and reasonable doubt. *American Philosophical Quarterly* 46(2): 131–140.

Vilhauer, B. (2012). Taking free will skepticism seriously. *The Philosophical Quarterly* 62(249): 8333–8852.

Vincent, N. (2013). Law and neuroscience: Historical context. In *Neuroscience and Legal Responsibility*, ed. N. Vincent, pp.1–24. New York: Oxford University Press.

Vincent, N. (2014). Neurolaw and direct brain interventions. *Criminal Law and Philosophy* 8: 43–50.

Vincent, N., T. Nadelhoffer, and A. McCay (eds.) (2020). *Neurointerventions and the Law: Regulating Human Mental Capacity.* New York: Oxford University Press.

Wegner, D. M. (2002). *The Illusion of Conscious Will.* Cambridge, MA: Bradford Books.

Wertheimer, A., and F. Miller. (2014). There are (still) no coercive offers. *Journal of Medical Ethics* 40(9): 592–593.

Xie, S., C. M. Berryessa, and F. Focquaert. (2022). The impact of Neuromorality on punishment: Retribution or rehabilitation. In *The Palgrave Handbook on the Philosophy of Punishment*, ed. M. Altman, pp. 441–464. London: Palgrave MaMillan.

Yang, M., S. C. P. Wong, and J. Coid. (2010). The efficacy of violence prediction: A meta-analytic comparison of nine risk assessment tools. *Psychological Bulletin* 136: 740–767.

Yang, Y., and A. Raine. (2009). Prefrontal structural and functional brain imagining findings in antisocial violence and psychopathic individuals: A meta-analysis. *Psychiatry Research Neuroimaging* 174(2): 81–88.

Zimmerman, M. J. (2011). *The Immorality of Punishment.* Buffalo: Broadview Press.

Cambridge Elements ☰

Philosophy of Mind

Keith Frankish

The University of Sheffield

Keith Frankish is a philosopher specializing in philosophy of mind, philosophy of psychology, and philosophy of cognitive science. He is the author of *Mind and Supermind* (Cambridge University Press, 2004) and *Consciousness* (2005), and has also edited or coedited several collections of essays, including *The Cambridge Handbook of Cognitive Science* (Cambridge University Press, 2012), *The Cambridge Handbook of Artificial Intelligence* (Cambridge University Press, 2014) (both with William Ramsey), and *Illusionism as a Theory of Consciousness* (2017).

About the Series

This series provides concise, authoritative introductions to contemporary work in philosophy of mind, written by leading researchers and including both established and emerging topics. It provides an entry point to the primary literature and will be the standard resource for researchers, students, and anyone wanting a firm grounding in this fascinating field.

Cambridge Elements ☰

Philosophy of Mind

Elements in the Series

Mental Illness
Tim Thornton

Imagination and Creative Thinking
Amy Kind

Attention and Mental Control
Carolyn Dicey Jennings

Biological Cognition
Bryce Huebner and Jay Schulkin

Embodied and Enactive Approaches to Cognition
Shaun Gallagher

Mental Content
Peter Schulte

Affective Bodily Awareness
Frédérique de Vignemont

The Computational Theory of Mind
Matteo Colombo and Gualtiero Piccinini

Memory and Remembering
Felipe De Brigard

Non-physicalist Theories of Consciousness
Hedda Hassel Mørch

Animal Minds
Marta Halina

Neurolaw
Gregg D. Caruso

A full series listing is available at: www.cambridge.org/EPMI.

Printed in the United States
by Baker & Taylor Publisher Services